WHO BOUGHT
JOE WILLIE
THE PRESIDENCY?

By

Wee Dilts

ISBN: 0-7596-8795-1

Library of Congress Control Number: 2002103479

This book is printed on acid free paper.

Printed in the United States of America
Bloomington, IN

1stBooks - rev. 03/22/02

ACCOLADES

Joe Willie; I thought was an amazing story full of political fiction and satire, splashed with an eerie sense of reality!

Watching the characters unfold kept me anxiously awaiting the next chapter to see what sinister plan they would use next to further their cause.

The action was fast paced and kept me turning pages.

Debbie Koscielecki

Another well-crafted story of good vs evil, Dilts casts an intriguing commentary on corrupt political beings from another planet, who plot to take over our government and then the world.

Joe Willie is a story filled with interesting characters; the evil doers are served a clever and surprising blow, and for once we can appreciate bureaucratic details.

Robin Labriola

Dilts has done it again, weaving a tale of interesting characters, fast paced scenes, and hints of morality.

Her characters come alive as they vie for the office of the president of the United States. She has captured the truly evil side of men who strive only for power and money. Joe Willie is a good read with a surprise ending.

Dorene Richmond

ACKNOWLEDGMENT

I would like to thank my friends who struggled through first, second and third drafts of this book. Their input, suggestions, and encouragement have kept me writing when discouragement wanted to take over. I especially want to thank, Debbie Koscielecki, Robin Labriola, and Dorene Richmond for their faith in my work and their contributions.

I would also like to thank my editor, William Greenleaf, for suggestions, corrections, and fresh ideas.

This book is the product of all of our efforts. We hope you enjoy it.

Wee Dilts

CHAPTER ONE

Ronald Best sat with the members of the Power Council on the massive wooden deck of the Baldpate Inn, looking out at snow-covered Long's Peak. The wings of hummingbirds purred as they hovered around feeders, and chilly air hinted that the birds would soon move to a warmer climate. To anyone passing by, the Power Council would look like nothing more than five businessmen having lunch and discussing their enterprises. Ronald smiled to himself; their discussion was much more sinister. They were planning to take over the world, populate it with their Generian race, and bring the remaining population from Nefaz.

Ronald Best was the leader of the Power Council, and he took pride in how elegantly he dressed. Today he had chosen a light gray pin-striped three-piece suit, with a red tie against an imported gray silk shirt. He fancied himself a fashion statement. Ronald had come to like the things money could buy here on Earth.

He sipped cognac, then spoke softly. "Avery says he has a boy for us who will be perfect as our Federalist president. He's ruthless, not too bright, easy to program, and can be charming. He can get elected."

The Republican Party had gradually lost popularity after the Supreme Court had placed George Bush in office even though he had lost the popular vote. The Federalists had immediately seized an opportunity to gain power, and now they stood against the Democrats as a major party.

Amused, Ronald watched Richard Rollins struggle to make his thin lips smile. He couldn't. "If he's five now," Rollins said, "how many years are we looking at before he can run for president?"

"Jack, show us the chart." Ronald felt the excitement of finally seeing this plan laid out with definite time lines.

Jack Ingersol, the statistician and planner for the Council, unrolled his flow chart. They all leaned forward to focus on the long-term plan for their party to take control of government and, ultimately, to save the Nefazians.

"We can run him for Senator when he graduates from law school," Ronald continued. "He'll be twenty-five or twenty-six. We buy him a Senate seat for twelve years, and by then he'll be around thirty-eight and properly married. We're looking at thirty-three years Earth time, which, as you know, will not be long on Nefaz. In the meantime, we build the party, bring in more of the Generians, buy them elections, and in thirty-three years, when our Joe Willie is in the White House, we'll own the world."

Samuel Gould chimed in. "I like the name Joe Willie. It's good for publicity—catchy and easy to remember." Samuel controlled most of the nation's newspapers and television news.

The Council member Ronald most trusted was John Woods. Nothing moved in the world that John Woods didn't have his hand in. He held controlling interest in war machinery, auto manufacturing, oil production, and weapon development.

"What about Janice Benton?" John asked. "She's been unstable since losing the baby. Will she accept adopting this boy?"

"Maybe we should have let her baby live," Ronald said. "She might have been more willing to take on another one. Benton says she's resisting the idea of adoption."

"I was against killing the kid in the first place," John said. "The doctor cost us too much. Human mothers are emotionally irrational creatures, anyway."

Ronald was about to answer when Ingersol responded impatiently, "Benton has been paid a great deal of money to see that she goes along with our plan, and then there's our guarantee of his governorship. It's his job to convince her. One woman's whim can't control our plans."

"I don't like her," Gould said. "In fact, I don't like any of these humans. She'll damn well have to accept this million-dollar baby."

Uncharacteristically, he had made a joke. Ronald stared at him.

In the ensuing silence, Ronald gazed at the other Council members in turn. He didn't like them. Yet each of them played a vital role in the success of the Federalist plan to move into power and create their Generian race. Thirty-three years seemed like a long time, and yet there was so much to do to prepare the way for Joe Willie to win the election. Once he thought about it, it seemed like barely enough time.

Taking a long sip of cognac, Ronald said, "I'll go get the boy, right after lunch. Who wants to drive me up Trail Ridge?"

"I will. We'll take my new Hummer." John loved his toys, and he drove only the most expensive.

The ship from Nefaz could slip in above the summit of Trail Ridge Road undetected; the thin air made it easy to cloak the vessel. Within hours, Ronald would be at the laboratory on his home planet, looking at the future president of America.

#

Joe Willie wondered what Avery was talking about when he said, "Joe, you'll be leaving us today." Dr. Avery was a human from Earth, and Joe Willie liked him, but he sensed no warmth or affection from the doctor or from any of the hairy Nefazians who tended the boys.

"Where am I going?"

"You're going to Earth to be raised by a powerful political family. Ronald is coming to get you… Ah, here he is." Dr. Avery left him to go greet the man in the observation room.

Joe Willie ran back to join the other boys in their game. He had no idea that one day he would run for president of the United States on the planet Earth. Today he played with the other five-year-old clones in the laboratory exercise room on the planet Nefaz.

#

George Blair ran as fast as his five-year-old legs could run. He still couldn't catch up with Matt, who was two years older. They burst into Representative Matthew Blair's office, and Matt jumped on his father's lap.

"We won, we won! I scored the winning goal. It went right by the goalie, kerwhack!" Matt was grinning from ear to ear.

There was not enough lap for George, so he went to the front of the chair and jumped up and down trying to get his father's attention. It seemed to him that Matt always got more of it than he did.

"I got the assist," George yelled. "I fed it to him. He wouldn't have scored if I didn't get it to him."

His father reached out and tousled his hair, but barely glanced at him. He continued to smile proudly at Matthew Blair II. "Matthew, they're going to love you at Colorado College."

George's enthusiasm died as he watched the two of them. He wanted to be a part of the camaraderie Matt and his father shared, but he felt left out. His mother said they were all alike, with dark curly hair, brown eyes, and chiseled masculine features. Everyone told him he looked like his brother, but he didn't think so. His father must not think so, either, because he liked Matt better.

As George turned to leave the study, he heard his father tell Matt, "Son, I'm so proud of you. One day you'll be a powerful man in the Democratic Party."

George left them and went to the kitchen. The scent of Hilda's cinnamon rolls drifted out to meet him.

Someday, I want him to be proud of me. I don't know what to do, but I'll make him proud of me like he is of Matt.

Maybe a fresh cinnamon roll would make him feel better.

#

Ronald arrived as the tangerine sun was setting behind ominous gray clouds that gave the planet an eerie green glow. Most cities on the planet smelled like sulphur, decay, and death. Ronald's home planet was suffocating. They needed to relocate to Earth soon to continue their work on the Generian race. The green fog rarely lifted, and many Nefazians wore masks as they went about the city. He didn't like coming here anymore. Earth living and cleaner air had spoiled him. But it was time to meet the boy William Benton would adopt.

Dr. Avery greeted him dressed in his white lab smock, his shoulders rounded from years of bending over lab equipment. Avery was always in search of new and more efficient potions to alter behavior. He had developed the serum that controlled the new Generians who made up the bulk of the Federalist membership. The serum had some flaws, but it was working tolerably, for now. Avery and his lab men were busy trying to improve it.

Avery had also been well paid by the Power Council to develop the human-like skins that Ronald and the other members wore, as well as the serums for altering human emotions. He had been responsible for the cloning of Generian humans, who later became elected officials on Earth.

Ronald nodded a greeting but made no attempt to shake hands or smile. "You said you have a boy who meets the Council's requirements?"

Dr. Avery nodded. "I think you'll find him more than suitable. He is without conscience, competitive, and not too bright. He's easy to program. He reacts favorably to the mood serums."

Ronald had hired Dr. Avery and hidden him away on Nefaz just before he was to be jailed for his work on human cloning.

They walked together to the gray building that had been set aside for cloning. Ronald didn't like Dr. Avery, but he liked the results of the cloning, serum development, and genetic breeding that were conducted here. The Generian race was predictable and systemized; they all fit the mold.

Light gray walls with a green trail line led them to an olive-colored elevator door. The hallway smelled of antiseptic and cleaning compounds. Dr. Avery motioned Ronald to enter ahead of him. "You're going to be very pleased with this one. He'll grow up to be perfect for the Council's ultimate plan."

Ronald said nothing. He focused on the floor numbers flashing by on the elevator panel. On floor thirteen, the elevator slid to a silent stop, the doors opened, and they walked out onto a circular viewing platform. Several technicians were there, watching a group of young boys playing a game in the room beyond the glass.

All of the boys were about five years of age and looked remarkably alike, with stocky bodies, curly brown hair, and thin lips that formed a straight line. None showed smiles or dimples as they played the game; it seemed to be very serious. One of them looked up and gave Ronald a cocky wave, then rejoined the game. The boy seemed to take great delight in tackling the runner and knocking him down.

His face clouded with anger when one of the other boys made a good run or got by him.

"That's him," Avery said.

Ronald could see he was competitive. Good, he'd need to be. The young boy looked up again at Ronald. A sort of lopsided smirk curled his thin lips as he attempted to smile. He waved again and dove back into the game.

"I thought we asked for one who could smile." Ronald had been making this request of Dr. Avery for some time. The new party members all had the characteristic thin, straight lips, incapable of smiling.

"You did. We cannot make them smile and still preserve the temperament you want. As smile capability increases, so does the capacity for compassion and joy. Joe Willie can smirk. That's as close as we dare come, if you want him to be ruthless."

Ronald intently studied young Joe Willie. "He'll have to do. We have no time for you to engineer another one. How does he take to the programming serums?"

"He does well. Give him humble, he's humble. Give him nasty, he's nasty. He's not extremely bright, but you wanted him for taking orders, not thinking. He'll serve your purpose."

"A human clone?"

Avery nodded. "We didn't think it advisable to use another species, so yes, he's cloned from human cells and modified DNA. I was concerned, since there are so many years between now and his run for office. If

9

he had to go to the hospital, I thought it best that he be human. He was difficult to create. You wanted someone people could like, yet you wanted him to be self-obsessed and uncaring. That's a tall order, even for us." Avery shifted his gaze to the floor and added in a soft voice, "He loves animals. Most of the clones rip wings off butterflies. Joe Willie tries to put them back on. He cries when animals are used in the experiments. It's just a little soft spot I'm sure he'll outgrow."

"He damn well better. We don't want a weak spot like that. Are you sure about altering his moods as needed?" Ronald was watching young Joe Willie with growing confidence that he would indeed be perfect, in spite of his momentary affection for animals.

"Yes, but flying him back here all the time for serums isn't practical, so we're sending Carl with you. Carl is a master chemist. Any mood you want your boy to have, Carl can create. One shot, and he'll be exactly as you want him to be."

"Is Carl one of us, or one of you?"

"Carl is a clone, extremely bright."

"Is he ready to travel?"

"He's ready." Dr. Avery cleared his throat and looked at the floor. Ronald stared at him with piercing eyes, anticipating his petition for more money.

"We did run into a lot of additional expense," Avery said. "Your specifications were demanding, and we ran into many complications."

"How much more?" Money was not an issue for the Power Council, but Ronald's eyes smoldered with anger. He hated being gouged.

"Fifteen million." Dr. Avery said the words as if he had said five cents.

"Ten."

"Agreed. When do you want to take him?"

"He'll go with me tonight."

#

Joe Willie busied himself watching the captain at the control panels. He was happy looking out the smoke-gray windows at the planets and stars twinkling in space. He had no social skills, so he simply watched and wondered where he was going. The man Dr. Avery had called Ronald Best didn't encourage him to talk, so he didn't ask any questions. He was afraid of the dignified man in his black suit. Even at his young age, he sensed that this man had power over him.

Carl walked toward the rear of the ship. "Mr. Ronald, I'm going to the back room to work on his mood formulas. If you need me, call."

"Can you create any emotion we want?"

"Yes, sir. Joe Willie usually operates in a self-absorbed state. He's not good at conversation, but I can create whatever you want. The shots last only a short time, and then he reverts back into his own little world."

Ronald waved him off. Joe Willie looked at him. They stared at each other for a moment before Ronald said, "I hope you're worth all the money we paid for you."

Joe Willie didn't know what that meant, so he turned to look out the window.

The ship descended to Earth in the vast Arizona desert, far from any major roads. Joe Willie, Carl, and Ronald rushed from the ship to a waiting helicopter. As the chopper circled and lifted off for the Benton ranch, the space vehicle quickly disappeared from sight.

Wow! This is neat, thought Joe Willie. He felt his stomach pulled downward as the chopper lifted off. Desert sand, brown, tan, and red, contrasted with the blue Arizona skies. Joe Willie loved it. The experience was totally new and exciting. He had never seen anything but the awful greenish fog that hung over Nefaz. He liked this place.

Ronald glanced at him over the top of the Wall Street Journal. Joe Willie could sense the man didn't want to talk to him, but he tried to smile at him anyway. Avery had talked a lot about smiling, and Joe Willie wished he could do it because it seemed important. He practiced in front of the mirror, but all that ever came was a pitiful smirk.

He turned his attention to the window, and as he watched, he saw the fantastic shapes of red sandstone rocks that were Sedona, Arizona. He could make out shapes of animals and birds. He loved animals and birds. He wasn't sure yet about humans.

The Benton ranch came into view, its magnificent Spanish-style home with red tile roof sparkling in the bright sunlight. The green lawn was a sharp contrast to the rust-colored sand. A sometime creek bed near the barn was lined with cottonwood trees. Joe Willie squealed with delight when he caught sight of the horses and cows. He had never seen such creatures, but he knew he was going to love them.

The chopper landed on the green lawn, and William Benton came down the steps of the mansion, shading his eyes from the sun. Ronald motioned Carl to take care of Joe Willie before he left the chopper.

#

"Well, how is he?" Governor Benton asked. Ronald could see Benton was anxious to meet the son he would adopt and help make president one day.

"He's fine. You have to remember, he's been in a group home, and he's a little rough around the edges. He has a sort of smirk instead of a smile, but we'll make it work. Have you convinced Janice to adopt him?"

Benton didn't know the whole truth. He had no knowledge of Ronald being from Nefaz, and he had no idea that Joe Willie was anything more than an orphan the Council planned to make president one day.

"She'll do it. She knows nothing about our arrangement, she only knows he's a little boy who needs a home."

Carl and Joe Willie came out of the chopper. Joe Willie was thrilled with all the new sights, smells, and sounds. He looked at the tall man standing near Ronald. He thought he might like him.

"Come over here, Joe Willie. Let me shake your hand." William Benton approached the boy and bent down with his hand extended.

Joe Willie looked at Carl as if he didn't know quite what to do. Carl nodded and made a motion with his hand. Joe Willie stepped forward and shook hands with Governor Benton, the first of many handshakes.

"Come on, son, let's go meet your new mother."

"I'm sorry, I lost my manners." Benton extended his hand to Carl.

Ronald introduced the two men, and they shook hands. "Joe Willie needs shots because he's hyperactive, and Carl will take care of his medications. Do you have a room for Carl?"

"Carl, welcome. Of course we have a room for you."

The four of them walked up the steps to the house. Joe Willie was so excited, he had to pee. Grabbing himself, he started to unzip his fly right there on the steps.

"Jesus, isn't he house-broken?" Benton grabbed Joe Willie by the hand. "Not here. Let me show you the place." He walked him to the powder room, lifted the lid for him, and left him alone.

Joe Willie came out of the powder room and heard the tall man telling Ronald and Carl to go to quarters at the rear of the house, where Carl would stay. Joe Willie watched them go and saw Ronald give Carl a large bundle of green paper. He would later learn that green bundles could get you anything you wanted.

"Wow, peeing in a nice white bowl was fun."

Benton smiled and took Joe Willie by the hand and led him across the red pavers to a large living room, where Janice Benton waited to meet the boy her husband wanted to adopt.

Joe Willie took one look at Janice and started running around the room, screaming loudly. He had never seen a beautiful lady. All he had seen on Nefaz were the nurses, and they were not pretty. He wanted to impress her with how fast he could run. He ran into a table and knocked over a vase of fresh-cut flowers. Water and shards splattered across the floor. Janice looked frightened, but Joe Willie didn't understand, so he ran faster and screamed louder, trying to impress her.

Quietly but firmly, she said to William, "Get him out of here. He's an animal."

Benton caught Joe Willie and picked him up as the boy's legs continued to churn. Benton took him from the room and closed the massive wood doors behind him.

"Carl, Ronald, get down here," he yelled. Both men came running. Joe Willie thrashed about in his arms, still screaming.

Carl had a needle in his hand, which he quickly jabbed through Joe Willie's jeans directly into his butt. Joe Willie felt the needle, and then he felt himself calming. When Benton set him down, he dropped to the floor in a heap.

"Jesus Christ, what have you brought us?" Benton sounded angry.

"Easy, William, easy. He'll be okay. He just got over-excited." Ronald looked at Carl. "He'll be all right now?"

Carl nodded.

Joe Willie looked up at Benton, his eyes wet. Benton turned to go to Janice, but Ronald stopped him. "There's another million in your campaign fund if this works out as we planned."

Joe Willie watched from the hall as Benton entered the living room and crossed over to where Janice was picking up broken glass. Benton reached down and pulled her up to stand facing him.

"Janice, are you all right?"

"What kind of a child is he? I don't want him. There's something very wrong with him."

"No, he was just excited," Benton said. "Janice, he's been in an orphanage. He just got wound up. You should see him now. He's calm and nice. Let me bring him in again."

"No. I don't want him."

16

"Come on, look at him now. He's calm. Please, Janice."

She hesitated. "Okay, one more look. If he goes nuts again, the deal is off. I don't think I'm up to a child like him."

Benton approached Joe Willie, who was still crying softly. He had heard every word and didn't want to be sent away. He liked this pretty woman, and she smelled good. If he wanted her to like him, he would have to be quieter. He let Benton lead him into the room. With tears gently streaming from his eyes, he looked at Janice and sniffled.

Janice weakened. "Come here, Joe Willie." She held out her arms, and he walked into them.

"I'm sorry," he muttered.

Janice nodded to Benton, and he left them alone, Joe Willie now comfortably cradled in her arms. Janice sighed as she patted his back. "It'll be okay, Joe Willie."

Joe Willie smirked. He had just learned a powerful lesson about tears and winning over women.

$ $ $

CHAPTER TWO

George Blair heard the whistle, picked up his hockey stick, and headed toward the locker room. Ritual called for the boys to moan and groan when it came time to give the ice over to the debutante figure skaters. Ice was made for hockey, right? Ritual also called for hormonal glances at the girls' long legs and perfect figures.

George Blair celebrated his sixteenth birthday this day. He and his older brother Matt were a pair, both olive-skinned with dark hair and impish brown eyes. Everyone said they could pass for twins. George enjoyed the attention they both received from young girls wherever they went.

Like twins, the boys' bond ran deep. Matt and George were much more than brothers. George glanced at his older brother. He loved him, and yet he had spent his entire sixteen years trying to measure up, trying to be as good as Matt so that his father would love him, too. They were competitive in everything. His father's political friends said they were both leaders, but it was Matt they picked for future greatness in the party.

The boys were muscled from years of privilege, sports, and trainers. They carried themselves with an air of being accustomed to having others do for them.

It was no secret that Matthew Blair, senior, had big plans for his oldest son. He would follow his father as senator, then the governor of Colorado, and then on to the White House. The party plan was in place for young Matt to run for the presidency sixteen years from this election.

"Silly girls," George grumbled as they cleared the ice. "Why do you suppose we have to have them, anyway?"

"Hey, little brother, don't you know?" Matt gave his brother a knowing grin and a teasing cuff alongside the head. He was already winking at the girls as they began to take the ice for warm-ups.

The Colorado College team practiced from eight to ten each morning. The coach allowed some of the more skilled players from the high school to work out with the team. George Blair was one of them. Matt was in his freshman year at Colorado College and would make starting line-up as right winger. George would be at the same college in two years and was already considered an expert defense man.

Slinging skates over his shoulder, George walked down the corridor toward the door. He and Matt were meeting his parents at the hotel for a birthday brunch. Turning to look back at a pair of retreating legs, George bumped into Judy Olson. He sucked in his breath; she was the most beautiful girl he had ever seen. Her blue eyes pierced him as he stammered an apology. He felt a change in his sweat pants he hoped she couldn't see.

"Sorry, 'scuse me. I didn't see you." Red-faced, he stumbled out the door.

"I guess you know why we have girls, after seeing Judy," Matt said, nudging his brother's shoulder playfully. George could tell all the guys were laughing, ready to join in his torment. He looked at the lake fronting the rink and flicked a puck out on the ice. They often played this version of chicken, and inevitably someone would run to catch the puck before it slid to the edge of the ice and into the water. The lake never froze deep enough for skating.

Matt took off to retrieve the puck, but he lost his balance and slid forward off the ice into the frigid water. The group was laughing and hooting at his plight as he surfaced and tried to get up on the ice. He went under and surfaced again, gasping and grabbing for something to hold onto.

George realized his brother was in serious trouble. Running toward him and dropping to his belly, he held out his stick. Matthew grabbed hold but went down again, pulling George dangerously close to the edge.

20

Team members grabbed George and began pulling him back from the gaping black water. Matt's grip slid away, and he went under. George was screaming and trying to move toward him. His teammates continued to drag him to the safety of the shore.

"No, damn it, let go of me! Matt, come on! Damn!" His cries brought people running from the rink and the hotel. Somebody was calling 911 on a cellphone.

George stared at the lake and knew that his brother was gone. Sitting down on the ice near the shore, he began rocking back and forth and sounding a primal moan. He smelled Judy's perfume as she put her arms around him and rocked with him.

#

Matthew Blair and his wife, Martha, were seated in the dining room of the Broadmoor Hotel waiting for their sons to join them when they saw their oldest son disappear into the water beyond their window. Matthew jumped to his feet, knocking over his bloody mary, and ran down the steps toward the lake, calling his son's name. Martha ran after him.

"Call an ambulance," the Maitre d' shouted as he, too, ran after the Blairs.

Hockey players formed a wall in front of Matthew Blair senior as he tried to run out on the ice. "Matt! Matt!" he bellowed as he tried to break through a wall of strong young men who kept him from meeting the same fate as his son.

Martha knelt down and took her hysterical son from the arms of a blonde figure skater.

Judy stepped back, tears pouring down her cheeks. One of the players held her. "I feel his pain," she sobbed. "Oh God, I wish I could take it from him."

When rescuers arrived, hotel officials convinced the Blairs to leave the ice. They led the shocked family to one of the finest Broadmoor suites and called their minister, asking him to join them and offer comfort. George was numb. He knew Matt was dead, and he felt as if it was his fault.

After several hours of searching, an emergency team was unable to locate Matt in the frigid water. The next morning, at the foot of Cheyenne Mountain next to the five star hotel, grappling hooks began the solemn work of finding the body of Matthew Blair II.

#

On a clear day, George could see Kansas from the Blair mansion, perched high atop the pink granite boulders of Cheyenne Mountain and nestled between blue spruce and tall pines. The Broadmoor Hotel was located directly below their house, and George couldn't look toward the hotel without remembering the tragedy that had occurred just three days before. He knew his father was suffering in the same way.

He ached as he felt the distance grow between him and his father. He wanted so much to hear his father say he loved him, but he got nothing. The two of them left each other alone to suffer their grief privately.

No one who was anyone had missed the funeral of Matthew Blair II at three o'clock that afternoon. The reception at the Blair mansion was now at its height, the men dressed alike in black suits and the women in varying shades of black or dark blue offering condolences to the grieving family.

Governor Blair acted as host, his brown eyes vacant and jaw clenched. George slipped away to the back of the house. Sitting alone, looking at the mountain, he smelled Judy's perfume as she came to stand behind him.

"May I join you?" she said softly.

He turned, his sorrowful brown eyes finding hers, his tears barely held at bay. "I'd like that."

He watched as she sat in the white lounge chair next to his. "I'm so sorry about your brother," she said. "We haven't really met. I'm Judy Olson."

Finding her eyes again, he offered his hand to her as he stood. "I know. Come with me, Judy."

He continued holding her hand as he led her up a path behind the mansion. The trail was flanked by stately spruce and pine trees, an afternoon breeze stirring their scent. Coming to an assemblage of pink granite boulders, he led Judy around the rocks to a small opening. He ducked his head and squeezed between two giant boulders into a large cave that looked out over the mountainside. They sat down side by side on one of the large boulders and gazed eastward, to the city of Colorado Springs and beyond to the Great Plains.

"Matt and I used to come here," George said, choking back tears. "It was our private place where we shared secrets."

Judy let him cry. It was George's first encounter with the awful void that death could leave in the soul.

Finally she asked him, "Can I do anything for you?"

"There's no one who can help me. I let him die." Again, tears welled up.

"That's not true. I saw you. You did everything you could. George, don't say that. If your friends hadn't pulled you back, you would have drowned, too."

Judy took him in her arms. He laid his head on her chest and sobbed the kind of uncontrollable, cleansing sob that every bereaved person must have at some point in the grieving process.

No words were spoken, but when they left the secret cave, he knew he was in love.

#

George stared at the ice. The coach said he had to start skating, but all he could see as he looked at the ice was Matt. He had been such a star—cutting, stopping, leaving guys falling on their butts as they tried to take the puck from him. George couldn't bring himself to go out and skate. He hadn't been able to do much these last few weeks. His only time of pleasure had been when Judy came by after school and they hiked to the cave above his house. Only when he was with her did he come alive.

He would never skate as well as Matt, and he couldn't take Matt's place in his father's heart. His father still ignored him. George ached for some sign that his father still loved him.

The old Broadmoor arena was just about done for; they were going to tear it down and build condos. He thought he heard ghosts of skaters past whispering in the rafters, and he shivered.

It was time for a decision. He went over the side and started lapping the rink, faster and faster. Maybe if he went fast enough, he could outrun the ache in the center of his being, the agony of his loss. *Matt, I am so sorry. I miss you. I wish I had gone down instead of you. Help me, Matt.*

He skated faster and harder, pushing himself. Tears poured down his cheeks. Finally, his muscles could take no more. He skated to the rail, leaned over it with his head on his arms, and sobbed. He vowed he would never skate again. That would be his punishment for letting Matt drown.

"Hey, kiddo, that won't do." The voice was real. He jerked his head up and looked around, but he was alone. Jesus, now he was going nuts.

"We need a man to carry on the Blair name. Dad needs a son. Don't wimp out on him. It's not your fault." It was Matt, all right, telling him what to do.

George was both frightened and comforted.

"I love you. Don't blame yourself. Step up and be the Blair son our dad needs."

"Hey, wait! Don't go."

The arena was silent. *Was that really Matt? Am I going crazy? I let him die, and now my father hates me. But maybe, maybe if I tried to fill in for Matt? Maybe if I tried to win back my father's love by being more like Matt?*

He would skate, he decided. He would try to become the Blair heir, and the next day he would ask the coach if he could play at right wing that season.

$ $ $

CHAPTER THREE

Joe Willie entered adolescence baffled and confused, as most teens are. But his self-gratification went beyond normal. He drank excessively, drove recklessly, and was totally out of Benton's control.

Joe was confused by his sexual desires. He kidded with the other guys and made girl jokes. He bragged about his conquests, yet he was most aroused looking at the male apparatus in the locker room. He had laid a couple of girls, but sex made him angry. He always ended his intercourse with angry, hurtful banging. He knew his money was the only thing that got him a girl.

He was sitting in the parking lot smoking with some of the guys when Marilyn sashayed past them, pointedly swinging her full hips from side to side. She was dressed in her short white cheerleader skirt and a tight-fitting red sweater. Joe Willie felt a familiar rise

27

in his Levi's. He ground out his cigarette and caught up to her.

"Hey, Marilyn, how about meeting with me after practice today?"

"Okay, how about under the bleachers?" She gave him a look and ran her tongue over her lips.

After practice today, she would quit teasing. Today he would have his way with her.

It was election day, and Senator Benton was seeking the governorship. Fifth period social studies would be spent talking about the election and watching the results come in. Joe Willie decided to cut fifth period; he was sure his father would win. Ronald and the Council had been at the ranch throughout the campaign, and they would buy Benton his governorship. Joe Willie was more interested in getting a six-pack and some Trojans. Best to be careful, since everyone did Marilyn. Today was his day.

He sat under the bleachers, hidden from the coaches by the equipment storage shed. He saved one beer to share with Marilyn.

She came teasing, her breasts thrust forward in her tight sweater, her hips swaying suggestively. He felt himself rise to the occasion. Marilyn looked at the nearly empty six-pack.

"Hey, did you save any for me?"

Joe Willie gave her his smirk and patted the front of his Levi's. "I saved the best for you."

She plopped herself down next to him, her overly painted red lips pouting. "You're soooo gross."

Anger surged through him, and he grabbed her by the hair. Pulling her over backward, he planted his mouth on hers so she couldn't scream. He reached up quickly to tear away her short skirt and panties.

He was in her in a second, pumping and pounding. She didn't really resist. Actually, she began humping under him. *God, what a stupid whore. She's helping me rape her.* Joe Willie pounded and pounded, wishing vaguely that there was some pleasure in sex. He finished and pulled out. *Shit, I forgot the rubber. Oh, well.*

She lay whimpering, telling him how great he was. Jesus, she was stupid. He opened the last beer, took a sip, and poured the rest over her face. He stood, buttoned up his Levi's, and left her.

He went looking for some guys to get drunk with. He liked guys better anyway. They were more fun.

#

Joe Willie knew he had a weakness: he loved animals. He was thinking about how he had begged Janice to buy Devil Dog. He'd spotted the cuddly black puppy in a cardboard box outside the market in Sedona. Joe Willie held him and sniffed his wonderful puppy smell while Janice gave the little girl ten dollars, and Devil Dog went home with Joe Willie. He loved the dog more than anything he had ever had before.

He was leaning on the corral fence throwing sticks for Devil Dog. The Arizona sun was warm, and the air smelled of cottonwood and sage. Joe Willie was pondering life. *Women are strange. I hate to have to marry one, but they say I'll have to soon. I'd rather just take a woman and not have to act nice and gushy just to get laid. Women want you to wear a nice tie and get all dressed up. Yuck!*

Joe Willie spat in the manure and thought of the white stallion down at McAfee's Ranch. From the moment Joe Willie saw the white yearling running free with his mane flying and tail held high, shaking his perfect Arabian head and snorting, Joe Willie wanted him more than anything.

Every day he went to McAfee's to visit the stallion. He named him Studder. He would put a harness on him and walk him around the corral, put the saddle blanket on him, and feed him carrots. He had been there every day for the last year, while he persuaded Governor Benton and Ronald that he deserved such a horse. He had to promise no more drunken shenanigans. Not a problem. He wanted Studder.

Studder was delivered to the ranch and turned loose in the corral. Joe Willie went to him, rubbed his pink and black velvet nose, and gave him a sugar cube. Devil Dog ran into the corral and barked softly. Studder laid back his ears and pawed the ground.

"Hey guys, we've got to all stick together, no quarreling among the three of us. Got it?" He spoke lovingly to both animals, and they seemed to understand. Devil Dog came closer, wagging his black Lab tail and smiling his Lab smile. Studder lowered his head to sniff him. Joe Willie patted both of them.

"Good dog, good horse. That's how it is, we three against the world." He could not have felt more love. The only time he had experienced anything like this gentle love was with the young boy he had played horsey with in middle school. He shook his head to chase away the thought.

Devil Dog and Studder did a little run together around the corral, and their friendship was born. Joe Willie vowed to quit drinking. He would be good and enjoy his two friends.

$ $ $

CHAPTER FOUR

Ronald took a long shower after his hunt, having gorged himself on a coyote. Now it was time to dress and go to the meeting with Benton. He laid out his forest green gabardine suit, a cream-colored tie, and a mint green silk shirt. Ronald enjoyed dressing in the best, and once he put on the human skin, he knew he was attractive by Earth standards.

Long's Peak stood as sentinel in the distance as a crisp breeze made the pine trees talk. It was a pleasant sound. The Council was gathered once again on the grand deck of the Baldpate Inn outside Estes Park. Governor Benton would be joining them for lunch. Ronald was excited; the time had come to lay out the final strategy, the flow chart of events that would ensure Joe Willie became President of the United States.

Joe Willie was now twenty. They planned to buy him a law degree from Harvard, not an uncommon practice among wealthy political families. Once he had his degree, he would run for Senator. The plan was to buy him two Senate terms, then go for the presidency. Thirty-seven was young to run for president, but time was running out. They needed to take control of the White House so they could move the lab from Nefaz and accelerate the creation of the Generian race. Every year Nefaz was becoming less inhabitable. Time was becoming a critical factor in their race to control the White House. Ronald felt good about the plan, however, and confident they would succeed. After all, they had more than enough money to buy anyone and anything they needed.

Samuel Gould interrupted Ronald's reverie. "It's been a long time, hasn't it?" He sat next to Ronald and looked out over the Estes Park valley. "I can hardly wait to see the blueprint laid out. The next seventeen years will go quickly."

Ronald nodded. The rest of the Council joined them, ordered drinks, and settled down to look at the long-term plan. Ronald was pleased that the Baldpate now served drinks. For years they had relied on homemade soups and breads. Now they hosted a first-rate bar, serving only quality name liquor and beer.

Ronald was the first to address the group. "Seventeen more years, and we will have our man in the White House. We'll have Joe Willie in a position of world power, and we'll control the world. It's our dream coming true."

"I'll drink to that." John Woods held out his glass, and they clinked rims all around.

Governor Benton came from the dining room onto the sprawling wood deck to join them. "I hope I'm not late."

Ronald pulled over a chair for him. "Not at all. Jack is just starting."

"Here's how it becomes a reality." Jack Ingersol unrolled an extensive flow chart. They all leaned forward to read it. "First, he has to get married. He has to settle down. His drunken escapades are costing us a fortune, and it's getting harder to contain the leaks."

Richard Rollins spoke in his quiet voice. "I have a man I want on the ranch to supervise him. Tom Lacy is a man of steel, a broken-down old rodeo hand, honest, tough, and with high morals."

Ronald looked at Rollins as if he had lost his mind. "What would we need with a moral man who might go running to the press?"

Rollins held up his hand. "Hear me out. He's tough, and he knows the world Joe Willie runs to when he wants to go berserk. Joe Willie runs to the rodeo to play cowboy. Tom can handle him, and he'll keep his mouth shut because he has a daughter who needs dialysis treatments and doesn't have money or insurance. We pay him well, his daughter gets her treatments, and we get his silence."

"It could work," John Woods said.

"It will work. I spoke to Tom. He knows his job is to baby-sit Joe Willie. He doesn't favor such a job, but he would do anything for his daughter. He's a good man."

Ronald looked across to Governor Benton. "All right with you, William?"

"I like the idea. There's a little foreman's cabin near the stables. He can live there." Looking at Rollins, Benton asked, "Can he handle Joe Willie? Joe's become an incorrigible drunk."

"He can handle him."

"Okay, let's get back to the plan." Ingersol was getting impatient. "We've found a suitable bride, Lillian Strom, daughter of Senator Strom of New Mexico. I've already proposed a financial arrangement to the Senator for his part in convincing his daughter to marry Joe Willie."

"God, that's great," Benton interrupted. "She is beautiful. How are you going to get her to marry Joe Willie? She's a class A woman, and Joe Willie is, well, he's a short, cocky jerk. And a drunk."

Ingersol smiled. "Money, Benton, money. Her daddy is bought and paid for. She'll marry Joe Willie. You're going to host a dinner party for every rich and powerful son of a bitch in Arizona and the surrounding states. The young couple will meet, fall in love, and get married. That's what we're paying for. The dinner party will also serve as a fund-raiser for the party."

Ronald was beginning to like this plan more and more. He could see it coming to fruition in just a few short years.

College, two terms for Joe Willie as Senator, and then a run as the Federalist Party candidate for President. Their candidate was guaranteed success. Ronald was sure there would be no stopping them, no matter whom the Democrats ran. The Federalists had more money than any of the other political parties. The Republicans were a joke. It would be the Federalists and the Democrats. Ronald smiled.

John Woods had a habit of summarizing their meetings. "So we get this Lacy guy to baby-sit Joe Willie, get Joe Willie a classy wife, buy him a law degree, buy him two terms as Senator, and then buy him the presidency. Is that about it?"

They all smirked and clinked their glasses. Joe Willie Benton would be president in just seventeen more years. The Generian race would rule Earth.

"Benton, call Janice and tell her to get out the priority guest list. Have her send invitations to all the rich and powerful in Arizona and adjoining states."

"Will do. Janice will take care of the details. She loves hosting a must-attend gala."

The plan was in place for Joe Willie to meet the lovely Lillian Strom.

\#

36

Ronald listened as Benton took out his cellphone and called Senator Strom. "Senator, this is Governor Benton. How is your calendar for a little trip to Sedona?"

Lillian's father wasted no time. "I could get there tomorrow."

"Good. I'll take you to lunch at Tlaquepaque."

"I look forward to it."

Ronald could tell the New Mexico senator was eager, as there was no hesitation in making the lunch plans. Benton would confirm the deal the Council had proposed to the senator: a hefty contribution to Senator Strom's campaign, one million dollars as soon as Lillian and Joe Willie were married, free press from all of Samuel Gould's communication holdings, and a guaranteed Senate seat for at least two more terms.

$ $ $

CHAPTER FIVE

It was the time of year when the aspen sent out their furry centipede-like buds, which would later become green leaves. The afternoon was lazy for George and Judy as they sat in their cave, holding hands and kissing occasionally. George hated that Judy was leaving for England soon. Her parents had given her the trip for graduation.

George was musing about his secret desire. He was a far cry from being a cowboy, yet he loved country western music and had always wanted to play the guitar and sing. He knew the words to all the classic country songs. Matt had been the only person who knew of his desire. He decided to share his silliness with Judy.

"You know, I have a secret desire."

Judy smiled coyly. "I know, but not here, not now."

He laughed. "No, besides you, and it's no secret that I want you. I want to learn to play guitar."

Expecting her to laugh, he felt his face flush. When she didn't laugh, he turned to her, and their eyes held.

"I think that's wonderful. Why don't you learn?"

"You kidding? My dad would disown me. Blair men do not play guitars and sing country tunes."

"Well, I don't know why not, if you want to."

"Hey, it's silly. Forget I mentioned it." Now he was embarrassed, and he wished he hadn't told her.

"No, I won't forget. Kiss me. I have to go shopping for London."

She moved into his arms, and they kissed. God, he loved her. They got up to leave, and George basked in the wonder of having someone who simply accepted him as he was. Her unconditional love made him feel he could conquer the world.

The next afternoon, when he entered their cave, he was surprised to find her there ahead of him. A smile spread over her face.

"Sit down and close your eyes," Judy commanded.

He did as he was told. He could hear gravel crunching as she scurried about the room.

"Hold out your hands."

He did, and she placed a large, heavy box in his outstretched arms.

"Okay, open your eyes."

Looking up at him from a new black case was the most beautiful cherry wood guitar he had ever seen. She handed him a book of guitar lessons.

"Oh wow, oh wow," he exclaimed. He was at a loss as to what else to say.

He picked up the guitar, strumming it tentatively, then began singing an off-key version of "Islands in the Stream."

Judy laughed. "I'm glad I'm going away for six weeks so you can practice."

"Well, I'm not that bad, and I'm certainly not glad you're going away."

She came and sat beside him. "I really don't want to go, but my folks would be crushed if I didn't. You won't forget me or flirt with other girls, will you?"

He looked into her eyes and said truthfully, "Not a chance. I am a one-woman man."

He tried playing another tune. "Oh, lonesome me…"

#

Cheyenne Mountain turned blue, then gave way to pink and rose as the sun climbed up Pike's Peak. George was lost as morning came to Broadmoor. He looked in the mirror at the full night's beard covering his face and ran his fingers through his tousled hair. He felt a sinking sensation in his stomach, knowing Judy was landing in England and would be there for six long weeks.

They had not been apart in two years, not since Matt had drowned. She had been his strength, his lifeline, and now she was in England and he was alone.

The Broadmoor Arena had been replaced with condominiums, and now the Colorado College team practiced at the new World Arena. As a freshman right winger, George Blair wanted to show everyone he was as good as Matt had been. He had trained hard his last two years of high school, winning hockey scholarships to Denver University, Boston, Harvard, and both Dakota universities, but he opted to stay at Colorado College because Judy would attend there in the fall, and they could be together. He took his lonely body to the shower for a wake-up and a quick shave, and then he would be off to the arena for his workout.

Martha was having coffee in the kitchen, chatting with Hilda. Hilda was the Blairs' cook and Martha's confidant. Martha was totally unpretentious despite the Blair fortune, and George watched her for a moment before he entered the room. He knew she preferred coffee with the help to sitting alone in the formal dining area.

She turned. "Hi, George. Have a coffee with me. You're looking handsome this morning."

He knew he was good-looking, but it was nice to hear. He gave her a gentle kiss on the cheek. She had recovered as much as a mother could from the loss of her oldest son, and he admired the way she had learned to show a face to the world that said she was holding it all together. He and his mother shared an ache in their souls that would never go away.

He was in a hurry, as all eighteen-year-olds are, but he noticed the deeper look in her eye that begged him to give her some time. "Sure, I always have time for coffee with my favorite woman." Beckoning Hilda to bring him coffee and juice, he put his arm around his mother and squeezed.

"I don't know about that," she said. "I think I'm only your favorite woman because Judy's in England."

They smiled at each other. Their relationship had grown stronger over the last two years, while his relationship with his father had grown more distant. Martha told George it was because his father had not stopped grieving for his oldest son, and that it pained him to look at George because he looked so much like Matt. He treated George kindly, bought him anything he wanted, but there was no warmth in his relationship. George knew his father would never again allow himself to experience the pain of loving someone so totally, only to have that person ripped out of his life. He wished he could bridge the gap, but his father kept him at a distance.

"Season tickets go on sale soon. Should I get some for you guys?" His voice was hopeful. He really wanted his father to get interested in the games, but he had not been to any of the high school games in two years.

"I'm sure he'll want tickets." George knew his mother was lying. She had become the salve to heal his pain. Lying for his father had become her responsibility.

George shared a quick coffee with his mother, then took off for practice. It was one of those warm days which might turn hot in the afternoon if it didn't rain. George looked at the blue Colorado sky and missed Judy, who usually came to the rink when he was finished working out. They would share a thermos of some type of health drink.

That day he skated as if his life depended on inflicting a certain amount of pain on his body. He did more laps than necessary, worked out on the bicycle, and pressed weights until he could do no more. He took a long shower and finally went outside to the place where Judy usually waited.

"Hi."

He whirled, surprised to hear a girl's voice.

"I brought you some juice. I know Judy always does, so I wanted to do it for you today." It was Evelyn, the cheerleader.

George sighed. "Hi Evelyn, that was nice of you." He put his gear in the trunk, wondering how he could get rid of her.

She came over and sat on the edge of the trunk. She wore shorts that revealed pubic hair and a tank top that showed cleavage and nipples. "Here, let me pour you some." She undid the thermos and poured both of them a drink in paper cups.

George took his cup and sat beside her. He gulped down the whole cup, then coughed and shook his head. "Jesus, Evelyn, what did you put in the juice?"

She laughed and poured him another full glass. "Just a little tequila. Do you like it?" She leaned against him, and he could feel heat radiating from her body.

He couldn't help himself; he felt the beginning of an erection. "I don't drink at ten in the morning." Then, for no reason, he belted down the second cup of tequila sunrise.

She was purring as she moved closer. "Today it's okay. Judy asked me to take care of you. She didn't want you to be lonely, so I have a little picnic in my car. You and I are going up Rampart Range Road for lunch."

"No, I've got stuff to do." George was uncomfortable and beginning to feel a slight buzz from the drinks. He could smell her, and she smelled good.

Giggling, she grabbed his hand and pulled him to his feet. "Come on, I've got it all planned."

What the hell, he thought, *I was just going to go sit in our cave and play guitar. Maybe company will be good for me.* After all, Judy had asked Evelyn to take care of him. "Okay, but just for a little while."

She reached up and closed the lid to his trunk, then pulled him toward her red Jeep.

He settled back as she drove up I-25 toward the Garden of the Gods, where they would pick up the

44

rutted gravel Rampart Range Road. He was sipping his third drink.

The road was dreadfully rough, so not many tourists traveled it. Evelyn handled the Jeep like a race driver. Dust and gravel spewed behind them as she sped up the mountain. George was glad they didn't meet anyone coming down the road.

Near the top of the mountain, Evelyn whipped off the road and into a hidden clearing. No one could see them from the road; they could look east over the entire city of Colorado Springs and all the way to the Great Plains.

George went to find a bush. By now he felt a little unsteady, but he was enjoying his blurred thoughts. It made the pain of missing Judy go away.

When he returned, she had spread out a lunch and another thermos of her magic drinks.

"Man, are you prepared!" He plopped down on the blanket.

Evelyn poured more drinks from the thermos as she leaned over him, smothering him with her cleavage.

They never got around to lunch, but when the afternoon was over, both of their sexual appetites had been satisfied.

As they gathered up their things, the Colorado sky was darkened by an ominous black cloud. Thunder rumbled through the mountain passes and lightning cracked. Hail and rain began to pelt down. George thought God was probably angry with him.

George had to stop several times to vomit as they drove down the rutted road.

#

Judy had promised to call him at seven o'clock. George waited by the phone in his bedroom, never too far from the bathroom. "Damn fool," he said to himself. He rarely drank alcohol, and was reacting violently to the tequila. He was disgusted with himself for being unfaithful to the woman he loved. Consumed with guilt, he sat on his oak frame bed and waited for Judy's call from London. *She can't see you*, he thought. *She can't tell by your voice, so relax. Damn fool.*

When the phone rang, he jumped, bumping into the night stand and knocking over a custom-made hockey stick lamp.

"Hi, is that you, Judy?"

Judy's laugh filled the phone line. "Why do you sound so surprised? Silly boy, I was supposed to call you at seven."

She sounded good. "Yeah, I know. I guess I was afraid you'd forget or get tied up or something, you know."

"How could I forget? I miss you so much. I don't think I can take a whole six weeks here away from you. You sound funny. Are you all right?"

George felt his stomach toss about, threatening regurgitation. "I'm fine. It's probably the connection."

"So, do you miss me?"

"Oh yes, yes. I miss you."

"Are you being good?"

"What do you mean?" He sounded defensive; he felt his face turning red. Guilt was an ugly friend.

"Hey, why are you so cranky? Are you being true to me?" Judy's voice was still light, but he could tell she was becoming more serious.

"Of course." Oh shit, he was going to throw up. "Judy, I've gotta run. We'll talk tomorrow. I'll call the hotel."

He slammed down the phone and ran for the bathroom.

After clearing his stomach of everything, he showered and went back to the bed. He picked up the phone, thinking he might call her back. No, he felt too guilty.

George hoped he hadn't lost her. Damn, he was stupid. He jumped into his bed and pulled the covers over his head. Then the bed began spinning in circles, and he passed out.

$ $ $

CHAPTER SIX

Ronald Best stepped out of the desert heat into the air-conditioned cedar library at the Benton ranch. He and William Benton were nursing Chivas on the rocks. Ronald glanced at his reflection in the window, admiring the way he looked in his navy three-piece suit, set off by a bright red silk shirt. No tie today, since he was visiting the ranch.

"I'm looking forward to meeting with Rollins' cowboy," William said.

Ronald scowled. "I just hope he can handle Joe Willie. We have to keep him out of trouble long enough to get him elected."

"He's been a disappointment to you, hasn't he?"

Ronald snorted in disgust. "That's an understatement. But we have to make it work, Benton. Carl can make him a zombie who obeys orders, if that's what it takes."

Ronald saw the red dust before he saw the beat-up blue Chevy pickup. Tom Lacy pulled up in front of the white stucco hacienda and stepped out of his truck. He was taller than Ronald had expected. Ronald watched the cowboy approach, noting that he hadn't dressed for the interview. Tom wore worn tight-fitting Levi's, a blue denim shirt, a worn cowboy hat, and a pair of old boots, all of which had seen their share of sweat and manure. He walked like a man who was in control of his life. Ronald thought Tom could be trouble.

Carl brought Tom into the library. "Mr. Best, Mr. Benton, this is Tom Lacy." Tom hung his hat on the carved wooden rack and stepped forward to give each man a firm handshake.

Ronald could smell horse and earthiness. He looked into slate blue eyes that didn't waver. He noted a small scar on the man's left cheek.

"Pleasure to meet you, Tom. What would you like to drink?" Benton went to the bar.

"Cold beer would be good."

"Glass?"

"What for?"

Benton smiled and brought Tom a frosty can of Coors.

"So tell me about yourself, Tom." Ronald got right to the point.

"No, let's get to the job you want me to do. Rollins told me some. Most of it I don't like, but as you know, I need the money."

49

It was apparent that Tom was not a man used to being manipulated. Again, Ronald felt concern. This guy couldn't be pushed too far.

Ronald stood so Tom would have to look up at him. "Mr. Lacy, your job is very simple. One, you keep Joe Willie out of trouble, and two, if he gets in trouble, you cover it up."

Tom stood up so he was eye to eye with Ronald. Benton stood too. Ronald thought they must look like three warring bull elk.

"Let me cut to the quick. You need a man to look after this Joe Willie and to clean up his messes. I don't like the job, but I need it. You'll give me a place to live, pay me a million dollars a year, and I'll keep your boy clean. Is that about it?"

Ronald exchanged glances with Benton. They were not used to such straight talk. Ronald downed his Chivas. "That's about it. I'll have my attorney draw up a contract."

"No, we'll draw up a contract right here. All we need is a yellow pad and a pen. My first month's salary is due in advance, today."

"Carl, bring me a pad and pen from the desk." Benton finished his drink and went to the bar to make a fresh one.

Ronald felt Tom watching them as a man might watch a rattler. He sensed that Tom neither liked nor trusted them, but he did need their money.

They drew up a simple contract, dated it, and all three signed. Benton started to fold it. "I'll keep this in the safe."

Tom walked over to him and took the paper. "No, I think I'll keep it." He folded the yellow page and stuck it in his rear pocket. "Now show me where I live, and then I want to meet Joe Willie." He picked up his hat and nodded to Benton and Ronald. Carl walked with him to his new home.

Ronald hoped they would not regret hiring him. He felt uneasy around such a straight shooter.

Ronald watched the two men leave via a new surveillance system which allowed him to monitor Tom from anywhere, including the barn and the ranch foreman's cabin. As Tom stepped outside the air-conditioned house into the hot desert air, Ronald could tell that Tom liked the desert, because he took a deep breath of the clean, dry air. Ronald figured the familiar horse, hay, and manure smell which filled the air made Tom feel at home.

Tom's quarters were protected from view of the mansion, but not from Ronald's surveillance system. Tom would have full scrutiny of the horse corrals and barn from his bedroom window. His living room faced out to the bizarre red stone sculptures and juniper-covered canyons.

Tom's log cabin consisted of a great room, a combination kitchen, dining room, and living room. A spacious master bedroom was accompanied by a large master bath, complete with Jacuzzi.

Ronald watched as Tom smiled at his surroundings, probably thinking of the hired help shacks he had lived in while he had ranched and followed the rodeo. Compared to those, this cabin probably seemed a castle. Tom made two quick trips between the pickup and cabin, and he was finished unpacking. Next, he hoisted his saddle on his shoulder and walked to the barn; Studder came to greet him, snorting and tossing his head.

The new surveillance system was the best money could buy, and the voice came through sharp and clear as Tom spoke to Studder. "I can see you're a spoiled one. Already you're begging for carrots and sugar." Tom fondled Studder's soft nose and forehead. He whirled around as Joe Willie's black Lab sniffed his pants and boots.

"Hi there, fella." He reached to pet him.

"These are mine. Both of them."

Joe Willie sauntered toward him with that weird smirk on his face. Tom stared as Joe Willie approached him, his shoulders hunched forward and up toward his neck, like a gorilla. Ronald could see Tom's amusement at this 5'9" man trying to walk the cowboy walk and show off his basket. Joe Willie really was a caricature.

Extending his hand, Tom said, "Hi, I'm Tom Lacy, and you must be Joe Willie."

Ignoring the hand, Joe Willie patted Devil Dog and walked to Studder, offering him a carrot.

"Get this straight, cowboy," Joe Willie said. "I'm the boss. You're the hired hand. Devil Dog and Studder are mine, so don't be snuggling up to them."

Tom sighed and leaned against the corral. Never taking his eyes from Joe Willie, he rolled a cigarette with one hand and struck the match by swiping it against his Levi's.

"How'd you do that?" Joe Willie asked.

Tom beckoned him over with a toss of his head and gave him the makings.

Joe Willie poured tobacco all over the ground and then a great gob in the white wrapper. By the time he had finished, he had a very fat, unsealed cigarette. He looked pathetically at Tom.

"I can teach you how to do that. I can teach you a lot of stuff, but one thing has to be clear. I'm not your hired hand. I'm my own man, and you and I are going to be like glue. If you're somewhere, and I tell you to leave, you'll leave. When I say jump, you'll ask, 'How high?' I'll pet any animal on this ranch, and I'll ride any horse, even this one." He nodded toward Studder. Tom walked closer to Joe Willie, their faces inches apart. "You understand?"

"Yeah. Hey, I was only kidding." Joe Willie backed away, nearly falling into the manure pile beside the corral.

"Good." Tom extended his hand again. "Let's start over. My name is Tom. Pleased to make your acquaintance, Joe Willie."

This time Joe Willie shook the hand. Tom gripped hard, and Joe Willie winced. Ronald felt that Tom could definitely handle Joe Willie. Maybe he didn't need to worry.

Tom went to his cabin. He said aloud to himself, "That Joe Willie is one strange dude. They're going to run him for the Senate? I think I'm gonna earn my million dollars." Ronald was pleased that the man talked to himself.

Tom called Benton at the main house. "I need to go into Sedona for a few things. Is my check ready?"

A few minutes later, Tom picked up his check. Leaving the house in his blue pickup, he turned off on a dirt road that might have been a shortcut to Sedona. Ronald knew Tom was a man who explored his surroundings, a man who wanted to know everything about where he was. A man who might someday need a shortcut to town.

#

One after another, the limousines arrived, winding up the dirt road to the Benton estate. From Arizona, Utah, Nevada, Idaho, New Mexico, Colorado, and Texas, every senator, governor, and member of the House came. Many political deals and conversations would take place this evening, none of them more important to Ronald than Joe Willie meeting Lillian Strom.

Joe Willie was in his room trying his best to get his cuff links attached to his white shirt. Damn, he was nervous. Women were for fucking; he didn't know how to make polite conversation with one. He sure didn't know how to talk to a classy woman like Lillian.

"Carl," he yelled, "get in here and help me. Damn it, Carl, hurry."

Carl came in with a syringe. Joe Willie held out his wrists so Carl could put on his gold cuff links.

"You look very proper tonight, sir."

"Yeah, well, I don't feel proper. What's in the needle for me?" Joe Willie was accustomed to having a shot to set his behavior.

"It will relax you and stimulate the part of your brain that comprehends social conversation. It will get you through the evening. Joe Willie, you cannot drink alcohol with this medication."

"This is a party! What am I supposed to do?" Joe Willie liked booze, and a party was for drinking. But Benton had told him that tonight was special, and he had to win over Lillian. Nothing else mattered. Ronald had told him that if he screwed up, they would shoot Studder and Devil Dog. Joe Willie decided he could get through a few hours without a drink.

Carl fastened one cuff link and rolled up the sleeve on the other arm to administer the drug. "This won't hurt, but you will get very sick if you drink alcohol." Carl plunged the syringe and emptied its contents into Joe Willie's arm.

Joe Willie waited to see how this one would make him feel. After getting his anti-drink shot from Carl, he finished dressing and looked at himself in the mirror. He wore elevated shoes so he wouldn't be shorter than Lillian.

"Carl, I don't know how to be with a sophisticated woman like Lillian Strom. How can I make her like me?"

He knew he sounded pathetic, but he was really frightened. He knew how to rape, and he knew how to smooch with rodeo fans and bar girls. However, he had had no practical experience with a real lady.

"You'll be fine. Just don't take a drink."

Carl opened the door and beckoned him out. He was finished dressing except for the tie. *A tux can make any man handsome, even a short guy like me*, he thought. He walked down the hall to get Janice to tie his tie.

Joe Willie found his way to the bar and watched the stairs for Lillian. He saw Lacy come over to get a beer. Damn, the man was handsome. Joe Willie envied Tom for his looks and confidence. He appeared at ease anywhere, and Joe Willie never felt comfortable anywhere, except with Devil Dog and Studder. He acknowledged Tom and sipped on his tonic water.

When he saw Lillian making her entrance, his chest constricted, his stomach churned, and he had a hard-on. This was going to be impossible. Then he caught a look that passed between Tom and Lillian, and he felt his anger and jealousy surface. His competitive nature took over as he summoned the courage to walk over and introduce himself to her.

He felt cocky and superior as he led her to their table. *Hey, Tom is just hired help*, he imagined saying to her. *I'm going to be the president someday.* He felt his smirk widen as he held out her chair.

He was fine until he felt Tom tap him on the back for a cut-in dance. He had been ready to take him on, but he kept control and walked to the bar. A beer would fix it. He asked for a beer, but was handed a near beer by the bartender.

He saw Lacy going for the door. *By God, I'll have it out with him.* He confronted Tom in the tiled entry. Ronald interceded just in time, much to Joe Willie's relief.

#

Earlier that evening, Ronald had watched as Tom dressed in the tuxedo Benton had rented for him. Ronald was amused by the way Tom talked aloud to himself; it helped him gain insight into the man. Tom wandered around the room, looking at himself in the mirror. Behind him were the pale log walls of his living room and a tan leather couch with a colorful Navajo blanket thrown across the back. "That couch and blanket look like they belong here, but I sure look out of place in this black and white uniform. I feel like an overgrown penguin." He smiled and winked at himself in the mirror. "This should be some night."

Ronald watched Tom roll one of his cigarettes. He sat on the porch to smoke it, obviously postponing his appearance at the party. "Well, tonight Joe Willie is supposed to meet his future wife. Rumor has it she's beautiful. Well, it's of no interest to me. My job is to see that Joe Willie stays out of trouble. Pretty women don't interest me anymore, anyway."

Tom ground out his hand-rolled cigarette and walked with long strides to the Benton house. The circular drive was lined with limousines and expensive cars. Ronald listened to the music and watched as Tom opened the door, joining the parade of dignitaries entering the house.

Tom went to the bar and asked for a beer, nodding to Joe Willie. Then he found a corner where he could survey the room and the staircase. Ronald was impressed with how sharp this guy was. He had picked the one spot in the room where he could keep a close watch on Joe Willie no matter where the boy went in the room. Senator Strom and his daughter were staying for the weekend. Ronald would ask Tom to take them riding into the red canyons behind the estate.

Ronald's hair stood on the back of his neck as he observed the electric connection between Tom and Lillian as they made eye contact. He had been right that there was going to be trouble here, and the trouble lay with this tall, fair-skinned woman with raven black hair who was descending the stairs. She wore a wine red, low-cut silk dress that revealed her perfect cleavage, a small waist, and hips that men would kill for. Her emerald eyes captured and held Tom's, looking dangerously flirtatious.

Every penguin in the room took a look, some boldly and others covertly, depending on where their women were.

Joe Willie moved forward with his characteristic gorilla walk to meet the magnificent lady. "Beauty and the beast," Ronald muttered.

Joe Willie gave Lillian his best attempt at a smile as he introduced himself. A genuine smile lit up Lillian's already perfect face. She stood a couple of inches taller than Joe Willie in her heels. Ronald was impressed by her beauty too, and he knew she was also smart. She had just graduated from the University of New Mexico, Albuquerque, at the age of twenty.

Ronald left the surveillance room and came to stand next to Tom, clearing his throat before interrupting Tom's reverie. "She is absolutely hands-off, Lacy."

"Yeah, damn shame, too."

Ronald stayed beside Tom. They both watched Lillian and Joe Willie go to their assigned table. Ronald smelled cheap perfume, and he and Tom turned to see a waitress from one of the local bars in Sedona who was often hired out for ritzy affairs. She carried a tray of drinks expertly around the room.

"Need a drink, cowboy?" she said to Tom. "You look hot." Her teasing smile seemed to bring Tom back to his real world.

"Yeah, I could use one."

"You look good enough to eat in that tux."

"Is that an offer?"

Ronald rolled his eyes as he listened to the exchange.

"Could be," the waitress said. "I'm off at one."

"Come on over. I'll buy you a nightcap." Tom gave her a wink and carried his beer to his assigned table. He had a seat at one of the round tables off to the side of the room, but located so he had a full view of Joe Willie and, unfortunately, an unobstructed view of Lillian, as well.

The music went from western to a quiet jazz sound suitable for eating and clinking wine glasses. The smell of filet mignon filled the room as the servers circulated soundlessly among the tables. Ronald continued to watch Tom. Tom could not take his eyes off Lillian. Even Ronald, who knew nothing of human love, could see that the man was hopelessly smitten, though he hadn't even spoken to her.

Ronald turned his attention to Joe Willie, who was giving sophistication his best shot. He wasn't very good at it, but he was attentive to Lillian, and she was gracious and smiling at him, except for periodic glances at Tom.

Carl sat down at Tom's table. "He seems to be staying sober," Tom said.

"I think he'll make it through the night," Carl replied. "He realizes how important his marriage to Lillian is to the party and to his career."

The dancing began as tables were unobtrusively cleared and moved back to create a large dance floor. Tom watched as Joe Willie took Lillian to the floor. He was not a good dancer, but Lillian made him look acceptable.

Ronald was seated close enough to Tom that he could hear him muttering, "What the hell, they won't fire me. They need me." That said, Tom went to the floor and cut in.

Lillian came into his arms as if made for them. Joe Willie glared angrily and walked away. Governor Benton lost no time in coming to the dance floor to cut in, but not before Tom and Lillian felt each other's heat.

"Tom, I heard some noise down at the barn. Maybe you should check the horses. Joe Willie is fine for tonight. Go on, get out of that monkey suit and relax."

Tom was dismissed; he had crossed a line. Ronald didn't think Tom gave a damn.

"Goodnight, Lillian, and thank you for the brief dance."

She smiled, her emerald eyes locked with his again. "My pleasure, Tom Lacy." Then Benton whirled her away.

As he crossed the crowded floor with long strides, Joe Willie intercepted him. "You stay the hell away from her." His eyes were mere slits as he spit out the words.

"Don't worry, Joe Willie, I know what has to happen here. Get out of my face, if you don't want to embarrass yourself."

Joe Willie looked ready to take him on, despite the five-inch difference in height and the thirty pound weight difference.

"Ah, Joe Willie, we need to talk. Good night, Tom." Ronald took Joe Willie by the arm and steered him into the library, where several party leaders were gathered for a strategy meeting.

"See you later, cowboy," Nancy sang out as Tom opened the massive doors and stepped into the crisp night air.

Jerking his tie and unbuttoning his collar, he took deep breaths to clear his lungs and calm his temper. "Goddamn it. I don't need this complication," Tom shouted at the night air, unaware that his words were being recorded on tape.

#

Lillian danced with many men while the caucus went on in the library. She was unnerved by what she felt for the handsome Tom Lacy. She had been in love once when she was seventeen, but this was like an earthquake. Somehow, some way, she would be with this man.

Joe Willie was a pathetic candidate for a husband. She had promised her father she would marry Joe Willie and become his first lady, but now she wondered if she could go through with it. Damn her father. She was devoted to him, and since her mother had died when she was thirteen, she had done everything to please him, afraid he too might leave her. She became his first lady, always on his arm at political events, turning men's heads and gaining him conversation with rich and powerful men. Now she was promised to Joe Willie and head over heels in love with a cowboy named Tom Lacy.

Joe Willie came from the library directly to her for another dance. It was more of a wrestle than a dance, but Lillian kept smiling and thinking of Tom.

"Would you like to see my stallion?" Joe Willie asked.

"Sure. I've heard a lot about him. Let me go change shoes." Lillian loved horses, and her toes hurt from Joe Willie stepping on them.

Lillian returned to the party in tight-fitting jeans, a faded blue denim shirt, and her cowboy boots. The formally dressed crowd clapped and cheered as she came down the stairs. She knew she looked good in tight jeans. She smiled and joined a stupefied Joe Willie.

They stepped out of the house into the night, and she took a deep breath of fresh, dry desert air. The crowd had thinned, and the musicians were packing up. Lillian knew all the deals had been cut in the library. She was here with her husband-to-be, and all she could think of was Tom Lacy in the log cabin near the barn.

She looked toward the cabin and saw the shadows of a woman undressing and Tom bending to kiss her.

Lillian reached for Joe Willie's arm and drew it close so he could feel her breast. She felt as if her heart would break. "Joe Willie, we're going to be married," she said calmly. "You do not have to win me over. I have no expectations for our marriage. I'll be a perfect political wife for you. All I ask in return is that if you have affairs, you keep them discreet, and I will too."

Joe Willie stopped walking. "I don't know what to say. I could love you, I think."

"Not necessary."

She tugged on him and kept walking toward the corral. Now she could hear Studder snorting and pawing. Devil Dog was penned for the night, or he would have been there too. They stood silently watching as Studder came to greet them. Lillian felt tears roll down her cheeks. She had made her decision. She would do what she had promised her father.

Joe Willie stroked Studder's nose. "Studder, this is Lillian. She's going to be my wife, and I told her she could ride you tomorrow."

Lillian knew this was an honor. Joe Willie let no one ride Studder.

They returned to the house, and she invited him to her bed.

#

Ronald felt as if he had rented a porn movie as he watched Tom and Nancy. They tried every position and technique. No matter what they did, it was no use. Tom could not get an erection. Finally, at 4:00 a.m., Nancy kissed him goodnight and drove back to Sedona. Tom lay awake, and Ronald was sure he was thinking of Lillian. *Damn, the Council didn't need this little complication either.*

#

Lillian heard Nancy's car leave. Joe Willie had been unable to have an erection. She had sent him to his room hours ago, and then she lay awake thinking of Tom.

She woke early that morning. She knew of Joe Willie's reputation for sleeping until noon, so she had plenty of time for a ride. She dressed in her Levi's and blue shirt, adding a dash of red with a scarf tied around her neck. She dressed with more care than usual to go for a ride, because she planned to see Tom Lacy this morning.

Janice Benton sat in the sun-filled kitchen looking out at the engaging sandstone shapes. The aroma of fresh coffee and apple coffeecake filled the air.

"Good morning, Janice. May I join you for coffee?"

Janice smiled broadly. "Oh, please. I usually have coffee alone. It would be nice to have your company."

Lillian thought Janice might be a terribly lonely person.

"I thought I'd go for a ride. It's so beautiful this morning."

Lillian poured herself a steaming mug of coffee and went to sit with Janice. She looked toward the barn, anxious to see Tom again. She didn't care if he was with that woman or not. She hadn't meant to fall in love, at least not with him.

"You and Joe Willie hit it off well, I hope?"

"Yes, we did." Lillian paused. "Janice, I know you know the arrangement. I'll marry Joe Willie because it means so much to my father. I may never love him, but I know how to be a proper political wife."

Janice nodded, and Lillian sipped her coffee, looking into the eyes of a woman she suspected knew a lot and kept most of it to herself.

"Lillian, you're young and beautiful. You might want to wait a bit and not settle for your father's ambition. You might want to marry for love." There was no bitterness in her words; she simply sounded reflective.

"I know what I'm doing, Janice. I promised my father and Joe Willie. I understand the arrangement.

I'll be fine. Besides, you and I can become friends."
She patted Janice on the hand and stood to leave.

"Enjoy your ride."

The early morning air was crisp. Lillian put on her worn straw hat and breathed deeply of the dry air, which carried a hint of juniper and sage. Her heart beat briskly as Tom's cabin came into view. She was surprised to see him sitting on the porch with a mug of coffee and a hand-rolled cigarette.

"Good morning, Lillian." His smile seemed to say a great deal more. His slate blue eyes brazenly looked her over from head to toe.

She knew her cheeks were burning. She felt like a school girl with a major crush.

"Good morning. I wanted to go for a ride, if you could tell me which horse to take."

"Why not ride Studder?" Tom stood and walked down the three steps to join her as she continued toward the corral.

"No, I just want a good trail horse, one I don't have to think about while I enjoy the morning."

"I'll ride with you, if that's okay."

"Fine." Oh God, yes, she wanted him to ride with her. She wanted him to be with her the rest of her life. Her blood raced through her body, and she tingled all over. *I hope I don't rape him*, she thought with a smile.

The sun began heating up the desert as Lillian and Tom rode into the magical sculpted canyon of red sandstone. They followed the creek bed, listening to the sounds of cottonwood leaves rustling in the morning breeze and eavesdropping on the canyon wrens as they went about their nest-building.

They rode in comfortable silence for some time. Lillian watched Tom roll a cigarette with one hand, and thought it the most spectacular thing she had ever seen any man do.

"Tom, we need to talk about last night."

She had to tell him that she loved him. He had to know, even though it would not change her plans to marry Joe Willie.

For a long moment, he said nothing. Then he calmly replied, "There's a place up ahead, a magical spot. You can see Sedona and red formations of every description. We'll talk there."

Shortly they came to the top of the canyon wall, where they entered a stand of juniper and spruce. It seemed to Lillian she could see forever; it was indeed a magical place. Tom dismounted, dropped a rein, and came to help Lillian. She needed no help dismounting, but she liked feeling him close to her. As she stood on the ground, they were suddenly in each other's arms, and their kiss reached to the depths of her soul. It was long, passionate and sweet.

She felt him tremble as he released her. He held her hand, and together they walked to a large flat rock, where they sat looking out at the red formations.

"Lillian, I love you. The moment I saw you, I was hopelessly in love." He turned and held her eyes with his. "But it can go nowhere."

Her eyes began to tear as his words overwhelmed her. "Tom, I'll go anywhere with you. I want to spend my life with you. I've never felt such love. Please, let's just run away to Mexico, Siberia, wherever."

"Lillian, no. You and I can't happen." He took off his hat and ran his hand through his hair. "I hate these people, but I need the money. My daughter, Tammy Jean, has to have dialysis treatments, and the only way I can get them for her is by baby-sitting Joe Willie. If I take you from him, the job will end, and Tammy will die. No, Lillian. We have to end it here."

She went into his arms and sobbed aloud. "Tom, it's not fair. I don't love Joe Willie. I'm not sure I even like him. I want to have a shot at happiness, and I can have that with you. Please, Tom."

He stood and walked to his horse. "Come on, Lillian, there's no way for you and me. It ends here. I'll always love you, but we can't be together."

He mounted his horse and held out her reins. She mounted, and they rode back toward the ranch in silence. Lillian was lost in her own thoughts.

#

Joe Willie rose early, for him, and dressed quickly in jeans, a red plaid western shirt, and old boots. He almost knocked Carl down as he ran down the stairs to the kitchen.

"Is Lillian up yet? I want to take her riding."

Janice turned to look at her adopted son. She hadn't seen him this excited since they had brought Studder home.

"She's already out. Left about seven. She thought you'd be sleeping."

Joe Willie felt uneasy as he looked out toward the barn. Studder's ears went forward. He was looking out toward cottonwood canyon.

"Damn!" He stomped out of the kitchen.

He glanced at Tom's cabin as he strode to the barn. He knew the bastard was with Lillian. He'd seen the looks between them. Joe Willie felt rage boiling up inside him like a volcano. He gave a shrill whistle, and Studder came running. Devil Dog was yapping and wagging his tail. Joe Willie quickly saddled Studder, and the three of them headed up the canyon along the creek bed. Joe Willie was furious.

He saw them riding side by side, making their way slowly back to the barn. He gave Studder a kick, and they took off at full gallop.

Stopping in front of Tom and Lillian, he pulled Studder up sharply, causing him to rear. Tom and Lillian brought their horses to a stop.

"Goddamn you, Tom, you leave her alone. We're getting married, and she's out of your league. I'll make her first lady. What the hell do you have to offer her, cowboy?"

Tom looked at Lillian, then pulled his horse alongside Joe Willie. In a low voice he said, "Cool it. I know what has to happen. She's all yours, though you don't deserve her. I'll leave you two now, not because of your mouth, but because I respect her. Joe Willie, don't push me too far."

With that, Tom rode away, leaving the two of them alone on their horses.

Joe Willie was embarrassed. He didn't know what to say to Lillian. He could feel his face turning red.

"It's fine, Joe Willie." Lillian hoped he couldn't see her tears. "Let's go back and talk to our fathers. The sooner we get married, the better for your campaign."

"Thanks, Lillian. I just didn't want to lose you."

Lillian sighed. "You won't. We have a contract. It doesn't include my loving you or being faithful to you. Likewise, you're free to have your indiscretions as long as they aren't public."

They rode back to the barn in silence.

$ $ $

CHAPTER SEVEN

George Blair was eighteen now and feeling all the mixed messages of a young man in love and in trouble with his woman. He slipped out early, hoping no one would see him. He made a clean getaway from the house and had a vigorous morning skate. George was not used to drinking, and his healthy body paid him back for the abuse.

Finishing his morning workout, he showered and dressed. He was going to go to the cave and play his guitar. Tormented by thoughts of Judy, he hoped that when he called her tonight, he could win her back. *I'll beg, I'll crawl, I'll do whatever it takes, but I don't want to lose her. I'm such a jerk.*

"Hi, there, you love-maker." Evelyn leaned back against her Jeep, her short shorts almost exposing her invitation.

He could see a thermos sitting on the hood of the Jeep.

He looked at the ground, then up to her breast, and he felt an involuntary rise in his sweat pants. "Hi. How you doing?"

"Really good," she purred. "I'd like a repeat picnic up on Range Road. What do you say?"

"Evelyn, I really can't. I have a doctor's appointment." He glanced at his watch to confirm his hurry. He jumped in his red Mustang and drove away. He could see her pouting look as he drove off.

Shit! What have I done? His thoughts went to Judy. He wanted to hold her right now. Well, tonight he would be really nice when he called, and maybe she'd not stay mad at him. He hoped.

The phone rang and rang. George could feel his own dry mouth, and his stomach felt as if it was being tied in a knot. "Answer, please answer. Judy, I'm sorry."

The line picked up, and a male voice with a thick British accent told him Miss Olson was out for the evening. Could he give her a message?

"Yes, tell her George Blair called, and to call me as soon as she comes in. It's very important."

He hung up and sat unmoving on the edge of his bed. If he lost Judy, he didn't know what he would do. Damn his maleness. He didn't even like Evelyn, and now look at what he'd done.

#

Judy had been hurt by his abrupt cut-off yesterday. What a fool she had been to think he loved her as much as she loved him. She was angry and hurt. The pains of first-love disappointment were overpowering. She decided that she would not take his call. Why open yourself up to more hurt? He was probably with some other girl anyway. She told the desk clerk she would not take his calls.

Sitting on her bed, looking out at the gray London fog, it took all of her self-control not to grab the phone when it rang and rang.

Judy called Denver University and accepted their scholarship offer. Her plans to go to Colorado College with George didn't seem to make sense, when he could forget her in one day.

Her female intuition told her George had already been unfaithful to her. She had made a vow long ago that she would not put up with infidelities like her mother had.

#

The next day, George finished his workout, and Evelyn was there again. What the hell, Judy hadn't returned his call. *She probably found some long-haired Brit to take her out. Well, two can play that game.* It made him feel better to make it her fault.

During the next six weeks, George spent many summer days with Evelyn. They always had sex, but never did he forget Judy. He wished he had never been such a fool. Finally, one week before Judy was to return, he decided to break it off with Evelyn. As soon as Judy came home, he would beg and plead for her to take him back.

He and Evelyn had come to this same spot up the dusty Rampart Range Road many times this summer. Today, as they sat on the blanket looking east toward Kansas, he said, "Evelyn, I have to quit seeing you." He was really ashamed of himself. He hadn't been man enough to break it off without one more quick sex session.

"Judy's coming back next week, isn't she?" Evelyn's green eyes filled with tears. "That's not fair. I've been really good to you all summer, and now you want to dump me."

He could hear anger creeping in behind her hurt.

"Evelyn, it isn't that. I just don't want to be in a committed relationship. I never told you I loved you, I never told you it was permanent. I just want to quit seeing you." He tossed rocks down the hill as he spoke, throwing harder and harder as he realized this was not going to be easy.

Her breast brushed his arm as she turned his face toward her. "Georgy, I'm pregnant."

George jumped to his feet, nearly knocking her over. "Oh, no, we used condoms every time. Oh, no. You can't be. Damn it, we were careful."

He felt his world stop rotating. A dull ache of loss, similar to losing Matt, came to him. If she was pregnant, then he could never be with Judy. George felt as if his life was over.

"I know, but somehow we must have slipped up. I'm pregnant. I went to the doctor, and it's true. Georgy, it'll be wonderful. I want your baby." She stood and put her arms around his waist. Leaning against his back, she rubbed against him.

"Take me home." He pulled away and began folding the blanket.

"Not yet, Georgy," she whined.

God, he really didn't like her. What a fool he had been. All he could see in his future was a life married to the town whore.

"Yes, right now." He left her no doubt that they were leaving, as he flung their blanket and picnic basket into her Jeep.

He jumped into her Jeep, and she drove them home. He didn't say a word all the way to his house. Evelyn tried every approach to get him to talk, but nothing worked. George knew he had to talk to his father. He called him on his cellphone. "Dad, I'll be home in about twenty minutes. Can I talk to you? It's really important."

"Nothing your daddy can do," Evelyn mocked. "I'm pregnant with your baby."

George glared at her, but said nothing. When she pulled up in front of his house, he got out, and without turning to look at her, he said, "I'll call you later."

Evelyn burned rubber on the driveway as she sped away.

His optimistic plan of dumping Evelyn and winning Judy back now seemed hopeless.

#

Matthew Blair sat in his home office, a dark-paneled room with floor-to-ceiling windows facing the eastern plains. His mahogany desk filled one corner of the room, and his law books lined the shelves behind the desk. A large conference table was centered in the room. This was where he met with party leaders to discuss election strategy and plans for the future Democratic nominee.

He was surprised when George called. His son sounded desperate. He had not talked one-on-one with George for a very long time. He could still not bear to look at him, he looked so much like his brother Matt. Blair knew he wasn't being fair to his younger son, but he'd not been able to forgive him for letting Matt drown.

Feeling old, he sat looking out the window. Sixteen years from now, he would support George while the party groomed his son to become the president. Few people realized how long plans were in motion before a man ran for the highest office in the land. He still missed Matt so much.

Matt was supposed to be the one. However, all of the party leaders agreed George could fill in and win the election four terms away. Blair should have been proud, and maybe he was. He decided he would be kinder to his youngest son. It was time.

He could hear George clearing his throat and tapping gently on the office door. "Are you ready for me?"

"Come in, George, and close the door."

#

George watched his father cross the room and add ice to his bloody mary. He was tall and handsome, and sent out vibes of power and wealth. He had graduated from Oxford, married Martha, and shortly became the father of two sons. He was a mover and a shaker in the Democratic Party. George looked at him, feeling a mixture of pain and pride. His father hadn't let him come close since the accident; George thought he still blamed him for Matt's drowning. He was sure after he told him what he had done, his father would hate him.

"George, I'm glad you're here. I've been wanting to tell you that the party has some great plans for you." Matthew Blair tapped the desk with a pen and finally looked up at his youngest son. He made eye contact for the first time in two and a half years.

"Come, George, sit. What is it you need to tell me?"

George wanted to cry. The first time his father had made an overture to him, and now he'd have to tell him what a fool he'd been.

He sat on the red leather sofa and hung his head so his eyes took in only the carpet. "Evelyn is pregnant."

"So?"

He cleared his throat. "I've been seeing her this summer."

"So have half the boys in Colorado Springs. Have you been screwing her?"

George was amazed. His father didn't even sound angry. He looked up and found his father gazing at him with a softness he hadn't seen for a long time.

"Yeah, yes, I have been. She says it's mine, but I was careful. I don't know how it could have happened."

"Count on it, George. She's on her back for lots of guys. You didn't commit to something stupid, did you?"

"No sir. I came straight to you."

He came from behind the desk and sat next to George. Haltingly, he placed an arm around his shoulder. The two men hadn't touched since before the accident. George felt good about his father's touch.

"I'll handle it. You're not to see her again, ever. No calls, nothing. Is that clear?"

"Oh yes, I don't want to see her. I want to get back with Judy. How are you going you fix it?"

"Don't worry about it. I'll see her father today. I'll take care of it. Judy Olson, she's the one the party wants you to marry."

"The party?"

"Yes, they have plans for your political career. So you get Judy back, and I'll take care of Evelyn."

Both men stood, and Matthew motioned George to leave him. George watched as his father went to the desk and began making the calls.

"Thanks, Dad." George turned, but his father was already dialing someone. George left the room.

Sitting on his bed, he wondered how his father would deal with Evelyn. He felt relieved, and now he began to wonder if the baby really was his. He had been extremely careful; maybe it was someone else's. He contemplated what his father meant about his political career. He knew Matthew had been groomed for the presidency. Well, it was time to think about Judy and getting her back. He loved her.

$ $ $

CHAPTER EIGHT

Joe Willie stood near the back of the chutes, drinking and spouting filthy words as he tried to pick up on the lady barrel riders who were preparing for their competition.

"I'd like to ride *her*," Joe Willie announced in a loud voice.

The pretty barrel rider heard him. She turned, and Joe Willie gave her his best smirk. Joe Willie knew some of the women found him attractive. His name, coupled with his wealth, usually gave him his pick of ladies. Most of them hoped to marry the Benton fortune.

Young Jeb Smith laughed so hard he fell off the chute, rolling around in the dirt and manure. He was nearly hysterical with his drunken laughter.

Jumping down to help Jeb to his feet, Joe Willie also fell. "Oh man, I'm feeling horny," he said. "Let's

81

go to your place and clean up, then take my truck into Gallup and find us a quick lay."

"Yo," Jeb said as he smacked his Stetson against his knees to clean it. He wobbled to his feet. "Sounds good. I got hot water and some whiskey. You got clothes?"

Staggering to his feet, Joe Willie gave the pretty rider a dramatic sweeping bow, nearly falling again. "I'll wear some of yours." He put his arm around young Jeb, mumbling, "I need a good lay."

#

Tom stood against the fence rolling a cigarette. He shook his head in disapproval as he watched the two drunks stagger toward Jeb's trailer.

He took off his hat and slicked back the runaway curl that fell over his left brow. Replacing his hat, he rolled another cigarette and watched the barrel riders. He remembered a time when his wife ran the barrels, and, as always, he felt an ache in his chest.

They had both been Rodeo Cowboy Association champions, he in roping and bull riding, and she in barrel racing. They were a flamboyant couple right out of a western magazine. Tom had even done some ad modeling in the Western Horseman.

"Hi, cowboy." A soft voice cut into his reminiscing. "Let me buy you a beer. Your young charge won't get in too much trouble."

Grinding out his cigarette with the toe of his well-worn boot, he turned, smiling at the familiar voice. "Shirley, that's the best offer I've had all day." He put his arm around her waist, and they walked to the cowboy bar behind the loading chutes. Tom heard the Brahma bulls bellowing as the cinch tightened around their flanks.

"Tom, you look good." She looked him up and down with obvious admiration. "You always were a man's man, and a lady's man too. That's a tough line to walk."

Tom smiled, embarrassed by the obvious compliment. "Flattery will get you a beer. And how was your ride? I missed it."

"Should be second, unless the new gal can beat my time." Smiling, she hugged his waist. "Can't complain about that, at my age."

"How's your sister?" He swallowed hard, unable to bring himself to say her name.

"Shelly's fine. God, Tom, you still love her, don't you?"

He opened the door of the bar, and they were blasted with the twangy voice of a country singer whose heart was broken.

"Probably always will." That was true, but not in the way he now loved Lillian.

#

83

Joe Willie and Jeb polished off three boilermakers before Jeb went to the shower. Joe Willie could see him from the sofa in the small trailer, and he found himself fully aroused. What the hell? He stripped and went to join Jeb.

Twenty minutes later, Joe Willie stumbled out of the trailer pulling on his faded blue shirt and yelling, "Jesus, oh, shit. Oh, fuck."

He was bewildered, even in his drunken state. How could a real man enjoy sex with another man? *I never enjoy sex. It's just a way to get off. Oh, shit, what if I'm a queer?*

His shiny red Dodge Ram Cummins diesel shook as he slammed the door. He beat a fist against the wheel as he turned on the engine. Gravel spewed from the tires as he floored the pedal. He had to get away from this place.

Throwing back his head, he let out a frightening howl. The sound was not human. He raced to the freeway ramp. He had to get home, had to shake this feeling of loving, really loving, a man. "Shit! Damn! I'm a man, not a fag. What would Lillian think?" He shouted out the window at the air.

"I need to get some action," he bellowed. "I need to get laid right now."

He took the next ramp and found a dingy cowboy bar next to a Texaco station. He had to find a woman.

Putting on his most charming smirk, he entered the smoke-filled bar. Most of the regulars were at the rodeo or at the cowboy bar next to the rodeo grounds. There were just two old Navajos, lost in their beer.

The waitress's large breasts edged over the drink tray. Her voice reflected years of smoking and smoke-filled bars. Her dull green eyes were hidden under peroxided hair, no longer seeing the people she served. "What'll it be, cowboy?"

"How about you?" Joe Willie gave her his best smirk. He thought he was going to be sick.

"That your best line, cowboy?"

"My wife just died. I need some air." He choked back a sob. "I need someone to talk to. Come out back with me. Talk to me." He forced a tear to go with his lie and turned his little boy look on her: sad blue eyes, brimming with tears, lips quivering.

Joe Willie knew somewhere at the core of this woman was a mother, a loving woman who would be sympathetic. Looking around, she saw that the two Indians had full ones.

"Sam, I'm takin' a break," she called as she took his arm and helped him to his feet. "Come on, cowboy, let's go talk."

Behind the bar, trash cans were tipped over. It smelled of rotten garbage and urine. Joe Willie put his head on her shoulder and cried. His tears were about his lost manhood, not his fictitious dead wife.

She held him and let him rock against her full breast.

Without warning, he threw her on the ground. One hand covered her mouth while the other reached

85

between her legs to pull down her pants; pleasantly surprised, he discovered she didn't wear panties. He was in her in seconds, thrusting wildly.

She tried to scream, but he held her firmly as he pounded away. Pulling out, he pummeled her face with both fists until she lost consciousness.

He ran around the corner of the building and jumped in his red truck, burning rubber as he tore out of the lot. In seconds he was back on the freeway, speeding toward Sedona.

"See, I'm a real man!" Yelling at no one in particular, Joe Willie felt better.

Diesel smoke spewed from Joe Willie's truck. He had probably ruined the engine with those two fast starts. *Oh well, I'll buy a new one.* He never heard the explosion of the right front tire. He was driving too fast and was too drunk; he had no time to correct. Joe Willie and his truck plunged down the embankment, still doing more than 100 mph.

Two drivers traveling west watched his truck leave the freeway. They both concluded it would be fatal for anyone inside the truck, at the speed he was traveling. They both called 911 on their cellphones, and, not wanting to get involved, both drove on toward Las Vegas.

#

Tom burst in the front door of the bar and saw Sam opening the rear door for Jimmy. "What's up, Sam? It sounded serious. What's the little shit done now?" Tom Lacy didn't like his job. He nodded to Jimmy, but he kept his eyes on Sam. The three of them went to a table, far enough away from the Navajos so that their conversation wouldn't be heard.

"Want a drink?" Sam asked.

"No, just tell me what happened. I saw the ambulance. Did he get in a fight?"

"Tom, you know I never bothered timing Dot's cigarette breaks. Sometimes she met guys, and sometimes she made a date for later. She was good about not abusing my good nature, so it was unusual for her to be gone so long." Sam glanced at the two Navajos. "Those two were grunting for more beer, so I went out back to get her."

Tom felt his stomach knot. He knew what he was about to hear was not good news.

Sam continued, "I found her out back, all bloody and moaning. I asked her, 'Jesus, Dot, what happened?'"

Tom knew Sam was a rough old-timer who had come to love his waitress. Most people would be surprised if they knew how gentle Sam really was.

"Well, I knelt beside her and cradled her head. I was afraid she was gonna die. I just kept repeating, 'Easy, Dot, easy.'"

Sam's eyes filled with tears as he continued, "Dot moaned, and I could see her pain as she realized what had happened to her. She closed her eyes, and I figured she didn't want to come back. I just kept cradling her bloody head. I told her, 'Come on, babe, you'll be okay.' Goddamn animal!" Sam banged the table, and the two Navajos looked up briefly before going back to their beers. "Shit, all Dot could do was moan. I figured her jaw was broken. I just kept telling her to hold on. Finally I laid her head back on the dirt and ran to call the cops. I made three calls—911 for an ambulance, cousin Jimmy, and you."

Tom looked over at Jimmy. He was Sam's cousin, a highway patrolman from Kingman.

"What exactly are we talking about here, Sam?" Jimmy asked.

"Not yet," Sam said. "Anyway, I grabbed a wet bar towel and ran back to her. It was awful. She refused to come around. Then they came, sirens screaming, lights blazing, the ambulance pulled in behind the bar. Good thing one of the paramedics was a woman. I walked around the corner of the building and lost my lunch. Goddamn animal." Sam clenched both fists and looked at Tom.

Two more patrol cars roared into the lot with their sirens screaming and lights whirling. Cousin Jimmy asked again. "What happened here, Sam?"

"What's it look like? The son of a bitch raped her." He wiped his mouth with the back of his hand.

"Who?"

"Can't say just yet."

"What do you mean, can't say? Do you know who did it, or not?" Jimmy was puffed up with his authority. Tom knew Sam only called him because he was family and could be counted on to do what had to be done.

Tom sighed, took off his hat and laid it on the table. Taking out his cellphone, he called the ranch. He had a direct line to Governor Benton, and this was not the first time he'd had to use it when Joe Willie screwed up.

One of the back-up men yelled from the rear door, "Hey Jimmy, we got a bad rollover just out of town. We're on it."

Jimmy jumped to his feet, straightening his gunbelt. "I'll be back, Sam. You'll need to give me a full report." He touched his hat in a salute. "See you, Tom," he said, and he was out the door.

Tom figured Governor Benton was probably reaching for the red phone to call Ronald before Tom even finished telling him what had happened.

"Stay there," Benton commanded. "I'll get right back to you. How much do you think it'll take?" Benton spat out the words angrily.

Acid churned in Tom's stomach as it always did when he had to do the Bentons' dirty work, covering up for Joe Willie's brutish actions. If he didn't need the money so badly, he'd take Lillian and leave. Then he would shower for a week, and maybe he could feel clean again. No matter, he needed the money.

"I'll find out. At least a hundred, I imagine."

Jamming the phone in his front pocket, Tom looked at Sam with blue-gray eyes, registering his disgust.

"I'll take that beer now, and while you're getting it, think about how much."

Flinging the bloody towel over his shoulder, Sam went to the bar. "Fuck." He threw the bloody towel in a corner.

Carrying four cold ones in his beefy hands, Sam gave two to the Navajos, then popped the tops on the other two with his thumb. He rejoined Lacy at the table.

"I don't want any money, but I want some for Dot."

"How about fifty, cash?"

"Don't know what being raped by a damn animal is worth these days, Tom," Sam said dully.

Tom winced. He hated this sort of dirty business. Sam was right. How did you put a price on that kind of degradation? The cellphone sounded in his pocket, and at the same time, the phone at the bar rang.

Governor Benton sounded as if he had taken a beating. Years of Joe Willie's shenanigans were wearing on him. "Ronald said whatever it takes. How much to keep them quiet?"

"One hundred for the barkeep, one hundred for the girl. Cash tomorrow." Tom had just doubled the price for rape, and it didn't make him feel any better.

"Done." Benton hung up.

Sam's eyes opened wide as he listened to Jimmy on the bar phone. "This is a bad one," Jimmy whispered. "I think his neck is broken, his head is real banged up.

He's barely alive. I wanted to check with you before we did anything. I think it's the young Benton."

Jimmy knew better than to follow official procedures when the Bentons were involved. All law enforcement in Arizona walked on eggshells when they were dealing with young Benton. Many officers had nice boats and campers that would be hard to buy on a regular salary.

"Get a lifeline chopper out there. Use a private company and a secure line, and stay off the damn scanner. I'll get right back to you."

"Should let the little fucker die," Sam snarled.

"Shit." Tom pounded his fist on the table, causing both of the spaced-out Navajos to jump.

Nearly pushing the number tabs through the back of the little cellphone, Tom called Governor Benton again. He repeated in hushed tones what had happened, then took a long swig of his beer. He put a hand on Sam's shoulder.

"Keep it quiet. I'll be back tomorrow with one hundred for you and one hundred for Dot." Tom left Sam to finish his beer.

#

Ronald watched the hands on the clock roll forward one hour. He knew in that hour a lifeline chopper had loaded Joe Willie, more dead than alive, and flown him to the Mesa Top Airport in Sedona. The crew was asked to leave the machine and the patient and to clear the airport. This was not usual procedure, but for a quick twenty-five thousand cash, who cared? They did as they were told. All flights from the Sedona airport were put on hold. The Mesa Top was cleared of everyone except Joe Willie and the chopper.

Ronald had ordered Dr. Avery to come in a ship from Nefaz. Joe Willie would need treatments far more extensive than doctors in Phoenix could give him. Ronald hated Joe Willie, but the Council had too much invested in him to abandon the project. He was perfect for their needs. Ronald had to smile at the thought of this doofus becoming president of the United States. Served the stupid humans right.

Ronald monitored the silver ship arriving from Nefaz on his closed-circuit surveillance system. The ship was cloaked so it was invisible as it hovered over the airport. Dr. Avery was aboard the vessel. A luminous yellow beam zipped to Earth, circling the lifeline chopper and lifting it into the hull of the ship. Once on board, Joe Willie was rushed into the operating room. The chopper was returned to the airstrip, and the ship spun out of sight, heading toward Nefaz.

If anyone in Sedona saw the yellow beam, they would be thrilled. The New Agers loved to tell of space ships coming and going from the area. They would have a great story to tell at the next cocktail party.

$ $ $

CHAPTER NINE

Ronald was furious when he arrived on Nefaz. He was tired of Joe Willie and his antics. Not only was the kid disgusting, he was costing them a lot of money, and he could cost them the White House. Ronald was panting hot breath as he stalked toward the green hospital building.

Dr. Avery came to meet him.

"He's really bad this time. His shoulders and neck are broken and he has a life-threatening concussion."

Ronald's eyes drew into slits as he spat words through clenched teeth. "Avery, I don't care about the details. I want him fixed. This is his year to start at Harvard. Fix him."

Avery took off his glasses and rubbed his eyes. "You really ought to let him go. We can make you another one. He's badly damaged."

"Goddamn it. We can't wait on another one. The plan is in place. Fix him." Ronald really hated stupidity. Avery couldn't seem to grasp the importance of the Council's plan. Joe Willie's march to the White House had begun. The Nefazians needed Earth. Their planet was dying. Time was rapidly running out.

"He was never really bright, and even if I can save him, he's not going to be the same. His brain is severely damaged."

"Can he remember a speech?"

"I doubt it."

"Can he be programmed, given shots, something? He doesn't have to speak for long."

"We can probably make up some kind of shot to get him through ten or fifteen minutes."

"Then do it. How long will it take? I need to take him back with me."

"I can't rush this surgery, he's nearly dead. It'll take some time."

"Bullshit. Rush it."

Ronald turned away, dismissing Dr. Avery. This plan had seemed so simple in the beginning, but Joe Willie was the worst one they had ever delivered, and totally uncontrollable. Well, by God, he would get some control.

Ronald looked at the clock. He needed to get back by morning. He sat down in the institutional green chair and put his feet on the table in front of him. Jesus, what a mess, and it had cost them another

$200,000 for the waitress and the barman, plus the bribes at the airport. It was getting expensive, and Joe Willie wasn't even running for president yet. Ronald was getting angrier by the second.

Nearly two hours later, Avery came out of the operating room. "It's not going too well, but we'll put him together the best we can. It'll be a few more hours."

"You've not been doing anything right lately, Avery. I wanted to talk to you about the quality of your clones. Dammit, Avery, you keep giving us the straight lip look. Can't you create a DNA that allows them to smile?" Ronald was livid; he felt his face turning purple. His own thin, straight lips formed a snarl.

Dr. Avery raised his voice in a rare display of anger. "I've told you and told you. If I give them the ability to smile, they develop an attitude of caring. There's a correlation. I can't change that fact."

"We pay for the best, and you give us babble. Avery, why can't they smile without becoming caring?" Ronald needed a drink. There was no liquor in this puritanical lab. "Another thing you could do is give them a sense of humor. Somehow they're not bright enough to be witty. We need a sense of humor."

"Why? There's no value in humor and wit. What's the point?"

"There's no damn value in humor? The humans, the ones who smile, seem to like humor. It gets votes, ones we don't have to buy." Ronald's head was aching. He really did need a drink. "Just do it, Avery. I don't know why smiling and humor are such damn problems for you."

Sighing, Avery dropped into a chair. "I don't know. We've run every test possible, and it just keeps coming up that smiles equal caring and kindness." Less defensively, he asked, "What's the problem? We've been turning out ruthless powerful men and women for you for years. None of them could smile. Why are you so concerned now?"

"Because people are beginning to notice that all the Federalist Party members look alike. The press and the cartoonists draw pictures of our straight lips and mean looks. It isn't going to help that our presidential candidate smirks when he tries to smile." Ronald got up and stretched. He needed to get back to Earth. "Work on it, Avery. We need Federalist Party members that can smile, and we need more women. The ones you've been sending are ugly by Earth standards. They look like Nefaz women. Give them bigger tits." He lowered his voice to a threatening level. "And Dr. Avery, make them smile."

Rubbing his eyes, Avery sighed and stood up. "There's no way. Smiling and compassion are linked. A sneer is the best we can do. I thought Joe Willie was what you wanted—evil, self-centered yet charming, and with his shots he can almost smile. Maybe next time," he muttered to himself as he headed back into the operating room.

Ronald paced and waited. The Federalist Party had gained ground after the 2000 election because George W. had been such a fool, the court jester president appointed by the judges. Americans were ripe for a new party, and the Federalists had moved in, building their Generian society. As they gained political power, the Republican Party was reduced to third party status, like the old Independent party.

Unlike other parties, the Federalists had unlimited money. They had started small, not going after the presidency right away. Instead, they started buying elections for representatives, senators, and governors in the western states, including Arizona, Colorado, Utah, Wyoming, Montana, Idaho, and Nevada. After that, they bought elections quietly, purposefully. Like a panther stalking prey, they moved into the Bible Belt. They adopted enough of the religious-right philosophy to win over the old right-wingers. They had built their power base, and world control was working on schedule. They needed Joe Willie.

\#

Twelve long hours passed before the operating room door opened again and Dr. Avery came out accompanying a sorry-looking Joe Willie. His strange gorilla walk was exaggerated because of his broken neck and shoulders. His head was bound in bandages, and he looked as if he hurt all over. He was barely conscious as Dr. Avery put him in a wheelchair.

"We did our best. He'll live. He'll walk funny, and he's lost some of his intelligence. But I think we can medicate and program him to get through speeches."

He handed Ronald a large black medical bag. "Here are some new formulas for Carl. He'll know how to administer them. Keep him in bed for a week or so."

"Shit, he walks even more like a gorilla. Not very presidential." Ronald turned on his heel and beckoned one of the hospital aides to roll Joe Willie to the ship.

Ronald called the Council members from the ship and gave them the word. No one was terribly happy about events. *Too bad*, thought Ronald. *They don't have to deal with all this hands-on like I do*. The salvation of the Nefazians weighed heavily on him today.

The ship landed in the middle of the Arizona desert, well out of sight of any major roads. The helicopter was standing by. Joe Willie was quickly loaded into the chopper and flown to the Benton ranch.

$ $ $

CHAPTER TEN

George sat in the cave and strummed his guitar. Somehow he had to win her back. He had been such a fool. His heart was racing. Judy was returning from England today.

Mrs. Olson had planned a dinner party to welcome Judy home and had invited the Blair family. George knew everyone was anxious to see him and Judy reunited. No one was more anxious than he.

As the sun set behind Pike's Peak, George showered and dressed for dinner. He paced back to the mirror, cursing his unruly brown hair. One rebellious lock kept falling over his forehead. He was on his tenth tie, but even this one didn't look right. He tore off the gray shirt and threw it on the bed, storming back to the closet. He thought only girls and sissies spent this much time dressing.

Maybe he should go casual. He tried black Dockers and a red polo. *Not bad*, he thought, looking at the smiling image in the mirror and trying to imagine how Judy would see him.

What if she didn't love him anymore? What if she had found someone else? What if she found out that he and Evelyn had had sex? Would she forgive him?

He looked awful. Maybe a suit and tie would be better. He ripped off the shirt and tried a navy polo instead. He looked like a bank robber. As he pulled off the black trousers, he realized he didn't remember which pocket he'd put the ring in.

His mother found him in his briefs, frantically turning trouser pockets inside out.

Martha laughed. "Lose something?"

Covering himself, he suffered a fit of self-consciousness, as if she had never seen him naked. He stumbled into a pair of tan Dockers. He felt the bulk of the ring box against his leg. Relief engulfed him, and so did his embarrassment. His mother must think him an idiot.

"Try the red polo." Martha retrieved it from the floor, handing it to her befuddled son. "She's not going to be looking at what you're wearing. She'll be looking at her ring." Martha had regained the twinkle and tease in her wide green eyes. They had remained dull for most of the two years since Matt's death.

"Thanks, Mom. Now, would you also ask her if she'll marry me?" he joked. Tonight he would ask

Judy to become Mrs. George Blair after they graduated in four years…

#

Mr. Olson greeted George with a hearty handshake as they stepped into the foyer of the Olson house. "She's in the living room. You kids take your time. We'll be in the family room having drinks."

Matthew and Martha left George and followed Mr. Olson to the family room. George threw his shoulders back, cleared his throat, and walked the short distance to the living room.

The sight of Judy took his breath away. She seemed more beautiful than she had been six weeks ago. A woman had replaced the girl he loved, and George was sure his guilt was written all over him.

She was sitting on a large powder-blue sofa, her dress of mint-green chiffon a statement of casual elegance. Her blue eyes locked with his. George was speechless.

"What would you like to drink?" She stood and walked to the wet bar. George watched her movements and thought himself the biggest fool in the world to have been unfaithful to her.

"Tonic. Plain." He heard his voice croak as he sensed her distance. *Oh God, don't let me lose her.*

"Sit, George." She brought his drink to the coffee table and motioned for him to sit across from her.

He made a bumbling effort to hug her, but she avoided him and sat down, crossing her long legs. He wondered if that was one thing he would be missing for the rest of his life.

She got right to the point. "George, everyone we know has already rushed to tell me you spent your summer with Evelyn. I suspected you had, and now it's confirmed. I refuse to spend my life with a man who's not committed to me. I loved you, George. I still do, but we're through."

"Judy, wait. Let me explain." Again he reached across the table for her hand.

"There is no explanation, no justification for sleeping with someone else. I won't live like that. I would always wonder who you were doing. No, it's over. I'm going to Denver University. I leave on Monday."

She stood up, and her chiffon dress cascaded over her perfect figure.

"Dinner is ready. Let's go join our parents."

"Judy, please, she means nothing to me. I love you." George found himself talking to her back. He felt the engagement ring burn against his leg. No way could he sit through a dinner with family. His life was over. The familiar sense of losing someone he loved washed over him.

She waited at the door and turned to look at him. "Are you coming?"

"No. Apologize to your parents for me. Tell them I'm sick. Judy, can we talk tomorrow?"

She found his eyes. He knew he had hurt her terribly. "I'll be there at ten in the morning. Don't expect me to make up with you. I'm hurt, George, and I don't want to be with you. But I'll come to the cave, and we can talk. Go home and take care of your upset stomach."

Judy moved into the dining room. George walked home.

$ $ $

CHAPTER ELEVEN

The aspen leaves were turning yellow, and a sharp fall breeze urged Judy to wrap a red plaid shirt around her shoulders as she went up the path to their cave. She could hear George strumming and singing softly his rendition of Elvis's "Love me Tender." In spite of her anger, she had to smile. She still loved him; that had been driven home when he walked into the living room last night. She had felt herself go soft and weak, but she would not be married to a man who slept with other women. She was still hurt and angry.

She stepped into the cave. George sat facing the entrance but hadn't heard her enter, he was so intent on his song. She stood examining this man who had broken her heart. He was dressed in tight jeans and a forest green polo. The familiar runaway lock of brown hair had fallen over his forehead as he bent forward, strumming the guitar and humming his song. His playing had improved, and he was actually quite good. His voice had matured so that it was sensual and deep, even a bit like Elvis. Judy shivered.

She cleared her throat. "Sounds nice." She had to fight an urge to run into his arms, forgive him everything, make up, and be with him forever. No, he had slept with Evelyn, and he had to pay for his infidelity.

He jumped to his feet and walked toward her, opening his arms to take her in.

"Judy, I was so afraid you wouldn't show up. Thank you for coming." His arms fell as she sidestepped his embrace.

"George, I told you last night. I'm hurt, I'm angry, and I've been betrayed by the man I wanted to spend my life with." She held up her hand to stop him as he came toward her and tried to speak. "Let me finish. Then I'll hear you." She looked past him to the hazy plains. The smell of fall was in the air. Black clouds were rolling up from New Mexico, and it looked as if it might pour later.

"George, I'll probably always love you. I was raised in a political home like you were. I grew up hearing about which senator, congressman or president was doing who. It's an immoral setting. Power lets men screw around, because most of the wives are as power-crazy as their husbands. They hide their heads, they look the other way, they close the master bedroom door to their husbands. I decided long ago, before I met you, that I would not live like that. I watched my mother turn to booze to hide the pain. I watched my parents play a game with their marriage, when it hadn't been a marriage for years. I want more. I want monogamy, and you've proven yourself incapable of that."

She couldn't help herself. She began to cry, and he knelt in front of her, taking both of her hands in his. Her flesh burned all the way up her arms. Damn, she loved him, but she was firm in her resolve not to give in.

His eyes filled with tears and his voice cracked. "Judy, what can I do? I'm so sorry. She means nothing to me. I was drunk. I don't know what happened. I was lonely. I was an idiot. Please forgive me."

Her anger replaced her tears. "Listen to yourself, George. I, I, me, me. What about *me*? I was lonely, too. If you hadn't hung up on me, I was going to tell you I wanted to take a flight back the next day. I suppose she was in your bed?" Judy felt her hurt and anger kick in. She pulled her hands away, stood up, and walked around the room, kicking gravel.

"Don't go," George said as she moved toward the cave entrance. "She was never in my bed. I got drunk. I was sick. Judy, I had to throw up, and then I was too embarrassed to call you back." He stood and followed her.

"Don't touch me." She looked at him. She knew she had to get away before she caved in on her promise to herself to never be with a man who was unfaithful.

106

As she looked at him, she knew why women put up with such infidelities. She would never love anyone as much as she loved him.

"George, I'm going to Denver tomorrow. I need some space. I want to date other men. We'll see each other at the games and on holidays. Maybe things will change, but I doubt it. I don't like the power you have to crush my whole life with your selfish testosterone-induced gratification."

"Judy, please."

"I'm leaving now, George." She turned and left the cave. The tears she had controlled flooded down her face as she crunched along the pink gravel path toward home. Then she heard the guitar and George's rendition of Hank Snow's "Lovesick Blues" drifting down from above her.

God, what have I done?

Judy went home to pack for Denver University's freshman orientation days.

#

George sang, he cried, he did indeed have the lovesick blues. How could he have been so stupid to lose the woman he loved over a summer of lusty, meaningless sex?

He stopped playing and put the cherished guitar in its case. He resolved, somehow, some way, he would win back Judy Olson. She was the only woman for him.

As he stepped out of the cave, the sky let loose with a downpour of rain and hail. Thunder rolled down Pike's Peak onto Cheyenne Mountain, and lightning cracked. George got drenched, but he didn't care. He was having a vision of walking into the White House with Judy Blair on his arm.

"I'll win her back," he shouted at the storm. "Do you hear me?"

$ $ $

CHAPTER TWELVE

Immediately upon Joe Willie's return from Nefaz, the wedding date was scheduled. One month of recuperation, then the wedding, then the honeymoon, and then Joe Willie would be off to Harvard to get his paid-for law degree. Lillian would live on the ranch, and Joe Willie would fly home for visits and treatments from Carl.

Lillian came to minister to him during his recovery—at least, that was what the press was told, and she did spend time with him. She read to him and tried to get to know the strange little man she had promised to marry. He seemed to like it when she read to him, probably because he was a poor reader and his comprehension skills were limited.

Sometimes she would look at him and wonder, *How in the world can these men make him a president?* She knew very well how it worked.

109

Politics was all about power, money, and sex. Money could buy anything, even the presidency.

She had been at the ranch for two days and hadn't seen Tom, although her mind was always at the little log cabin hidden from the main house. She had seen his blue pickup going by the house, and she noticed he usually took a ride up the canyon at sunset. Tonight, the sun was painting the sandstone a deep red, and a crisp fall breeze stirred the cottonwoods along the creek bed. The leaves had turned a rusty shade of orange. Joe Willie was asleep. Everyone else had gone to Phoenix for a fund-raiser.

Lillian rushed to the barn. Tom was saddling his roan for an evening ride. "How about company?" she heard her own husky voice say.

Tom turned, and a smile lit his face and eyes. The heat of their love was immediately ignited. "Sure, you want Studder?"

"No. It doesn't seem right to ride his favorite horse when I want to be with the man I love."

"Jesus, Lillian. Stop that. We can ride together, but that's it. This thing between us has to be kept in check."

She smiled as she noticed a change in the front of Tom's tight Levi's. "Right. I'll ride the pinto."

As they rode up the canyon, Tom rolled a one-handed cigarette. Lillian still thought that was the sexiest thing she had ever seen a man do. Comfortable with the silence, they rode to the top of the canyon and watched the sun setting on Sedona.

"Tom, I have a contract, an arrangement, if you will, with Joe Willie. I have a duty to help get him elected. I've sold out so my Father can stay in office. It's how the game is played. But I'm free to come to you as long as we keep a low profile."

Tom hung his head and took off his hat, setting it on the rock beside him. He sighed mightily before turning to look into her eyes. The look was so intense, Lillian felt as if he could see into her soul.

"Lillian, I have never loved as I love you. My God, the first time I saw you, I thought a Mack truck had run me over. But I cannot lose this job. Tammy Jean's life depends on her treatments, and they're expensive."

She knelt on the ground in front of him, taking his hands in hers, "I know. We'll be careful. I have to have you in my life."

With that she raised her lips to his, and he bent to meet her. They consummated their love on the red sandstone of the mesa. The chilly desert breeze did not faze their heat.

Riding back to the ranch, they talked of their lives, their dreams, and how life had taken them in many different directions. Lillian had never been so fulfilled and so much in love.

"Tom, I'll come as often as I can. Probably every night." She chuckled.

"Fine by me. My God, I'm so glad you're here."

"Me, too. Roll a cigarette for me."

"You smoke?"

"No, but you make it look so sexy."

Tom laughed and rolled a cigarette for each of them. Lillian coughed and sputtered as she dragged a lungful of strong tobacco.

They were both laughing as they reached the stable and began unsaddling their horses. Neither of them saw Joe Willie limping back to the house.

#

Lillian showered and ate a salad before knocking on Joe Willie's door. "You awake?" She entered his room and was shocked by the animal anger that flared in his eyes.

"Was he good, Lillian?" he snarled, his mouth tight and eyes narrowed to slits.

Lillian felt reciprocal anger. *What a prick! Did he think she would be here if it weren't for the deal?* "Hey, I told you from the beginning. We have a contract. I don't love you now and never will. I'll be good for your political career. You can drink and fuck all you want. Just keep it private. In public I'll be your devoted spouse, but in private I'll do whatever I damn well please. So cool it, little man."

She turned and left the room, slamming the solid oak door so hard Carl came running from his room across the hall.

"Is he okay?"

"Yes. But he needs his ego taken down a notch, and maybe you could give him a shot of intelligence!"

Lillian went to her room, undressed, and put a red chiffon robe over her naked body. It was a short walk to Tom's cabin. He took her in his arms, and instantly they were lost in the passion of newfound love.

#

Three weeks had passed when Joe Willie took off for Sedona. About three in the afternoon, he roared up the drive in his brand new red Dodge Ram pickup, complete with naked-lady hood ornament. Slamming the brakes, he came to an ear-splitting stop. Joe Willie felt a little woozy as he stepped from his truck.

"Hi, my boy," he slurred as Devil Dog came running, yapping and fiercely wagging his tail. Joe Willie fell over as he squatted to pet his beloved friend. Devil Dog licked his face as they rolled on the lawn beside the driveway.

He could see Lillian watching him from the house. Tonight he would get her. He would force her to have sex with him. Drinking made him feel like a real man.

#

Ronald and William Benton watched the drunken scene.

"Senator, you're going to have to do something about his drinking. It's time to get his law degree, and we need to groom him for his political career. He has to get some control."

Ronald had come to hate Joe Willie. It didn't matter how much money they spent covering up his shenanigans, or how many personalized shots they concocted for him, he simply remained out of control.

William poured himself two fingers of Cutty. "I'm afraid it's going to take a lot of grooming. His drinking is beyond control."

"Then we'll develop new shots, we'll send him to the rehabilitation center in Sedona, and if that doesn't work, I'll kill that damned stallion."

"I don't know if we can get him through college. He seems slower since the accident. I can't get him to talk sense. How will he be able to study, go to classes, and pass tests?"

As Ronald looked out the window, his stomach knotted. He jabbed the intercom button to Carl's apartment.

"Carl, Joe Willie is out front, and he's drunk. Give him a shot and bring him in here."

He watched as Carl went outside and deftly give Joe Willie a shot through the sleeve of his faded denim shirt, then put an arm around him and helped him walk to the house.

How many millions had they spent? Too many. But it was too late to replace him. Twenty-one years, and now he needed to start making his moves to get a law degree, run a successful Senate campaign, and in twelve years be ready to run for the presidency. They had bought and paid for everything. *I'll be damned if*

I'll let this drunken jerk ruin our plans. Ronald's thoughts raced as he waited for Carl and Joe Willie.

Carl half-carried Joe Willie into the oak-paneled library, settling his limp frame onto the red leather couch. Ronald could smell him from across the room, reeking of booze and smoke. Ronald stalked across the room and jerked the boy's head up by the hair.

"Listen to me, you little asshole."

Joe Willie was coming awake, the shots bringing him from drunkenness to lucidity in a matter of seconds.

"Yo, Mr. Ronald." His slurred speech was improving. He gave Ronald his sickly smirk.

"Don't 'yo' me." Ronald pulled Joe Willie to a standing position and walked him to the window, where they could both see the corral.

Studder was trotting around the corral, tossing his magnificent head and snorting. Devil Dog was yapping as he ran with him. The two had formed a unique friendship and often played together as they were now.

"Take a good look at your horse, Joe Willie. I'm telling you, if you don't shape up, I'm going to kill both the horse and the dog."

"No!" Joe Willie wailed. "No, I'll do whatever you ask. Please don't hurt Studder and Devil Dog."

"I won't hurt them. I'll kill them. Now listen up. Carl is going to take you to the dry-out center in Sedona. All you have to do is stay clean and sober for thirty days. You're starting college next month. I'm not kidding you, if you slip up again, your horse and dog are dead."

He let go of Joe Willie's head and walked to the huge oak doors. He turned to William Benton. "You get him sober. I'll be back with the committee in thirty days. I want him dried out. His campaign begins when he enters Harvard, thirty days from today. Marrying Lillian was step one, entering Harvard is step two. Get him sober." The door slammed behind him.

#

The shot and Ronald's threats had sobered him. Joe Willie went to the barn and saddled Studder.

"Studder boy, we need to go for a ride." He caressed the soft pink and black nose. Studder snorted and tossed his head, and Devil Dog wagged his tail and barked.

Mounting his magnificent horse, Joe Willie took Devil Dog and rode into the beautiful red canyon. They rode through the spruce and juniper, Joe Willie breathing in the smells and listening to the sounds of the canyon wrens. He had a special place way up in the canyon at the top of the ridge, where he could see Sedona and the valley floor. This was the only place where Joe Willie felt peace.

He sat on a rock and looked out at the desert he loved. Devil Dog nosed himself under a hand for petting. Studder nuzzled his shoulder.

"I love you guys. I wish I could love people like I do you, but they don't understand me. I feel so damn alone."

He tore off a branch of juniper bush and began munching on the needles, wondering how he could stay sober.

"When I'm drinking is the only time I feel good, except the times I come out here with you. I can't let them hurt you, and I can't do what they ask. I can't even make conversation, let alone speeches. Hey, maybe we three ought to just run off."

Joe Willie felt trapped in a game not of his making. "Okay, I really will try to stay sober and do what they want. I don't know what else to do. I want to protect you, so I'll try. Come on, let's go back, and I'll go to the rehab center and see if I can get clean and sober."

He mounted Studder, and the three of them trotted back to the barn.

$ $ $

CHAPTER THIRTEEN

Now George could barely get through the crack formed by the pink granite rocks. This opening led to a small cave that faced north and west, where he and Matt had played when they were boys. He hadn't gone to the secret place in years, not since Matt had died. From here, he could see the Garden of the Gods, with its majestic rock formations jutting up from the valley floor. To the west he could see Ute Pass and Pike's Peak. Somehow this spot seemed sacred to him. Maybe it was the beauty of the landscape, or perhaps the ancient spirit of the Utes. He felt as good in this place as he had six years before.

"Hey, I got an idea." He heard Matt as if it were yesterday.

"Yeah, what is it?" George was always eager to please his older brother.

"This is going to be our Indian sweat room."

"What's that?" George had always been in awe of all the things his fourteen-year-old brother knew.

"It's where you go to meditate and get visions, stuff like that."

George smiled at the memory and looked out at the view. *I need a vision. I'm so confused.*

George and Judy were both finishing up their senior years, getting ready to move on to graduate school. During the past three and a half years, they had become best friends. They didn't date, but not because he didn't ask every time he saw her. Judy refused to be his girlfriend. They saw each other at Denver University and Colorado College hockey games, and, if possible, they had dinner together either before or after the game. On holidays, when Judy came home, they would see each other at parties, and once in a while they went to a movie. But they were never intimate. George still wanted her more than anything in life. She was coming home for Christmas, and he was going to talk to her about getting back together and ask her to help with his decision.

The Democratic Party had laid out a political proposal. He was to get a law degree, pass the bar, win two terms as senator, then run for president. He knew his father wanted him to take it. *I would like to be politically involved. I think I could do something good for my country. But I'd also like to goof around and play professional hockey.*

"Still looking for the magic answer, little brother?"

George bolted up from his rock and spun around. He could not see Matt, but he surely heard him.

"Matt?"

"Yes. George, the hockey contract: five million a year for five years for a rookie player? Unheard of. Lots of temptation there, right?"

"Uh, yeah." George was still looking around the room, trying to see where the voice came from.

"President, with Judy on your arm as first lady sounds good, too?"

"Matt, dammit, show yourself. You're making me crazy."

Matt's familiar laugh echoed in the small room. "Not a chance. I have to get back. George, you know what to do. Listen to your soul, stop trying to please Father. You'll never be his first son. Find out who you are and become that man."

He was gone. George sat down, disconcerted by the experience. Had it been real? Did Matt really watch over him, or was he just a little crazy?

He ran down the gravel tree-lined trail, his heart racing as it always did when he was going to see or talk to Judy. He dashed to his room and dialed her number. *Please be there, please.*

"Hi, Judy here." Her voice sounded so good.

"Hi, George here. Judy, when are you getting into Springs?"

"Tonight. Why, what's the matter?"

"Nothing is the matter, but you have to have dinner with me tonight. Broadmoor, eight o'clock. I'll pick you up. I won't take no for an answer."

He heard her laugh. "Okay, George. I'll be ready."

George threw his fist in the air. "Yes!"

Martha stuck her head in the door. "You all right?"

He ran over and hugged his mother. "Yes, Judy is going to dinner with me tonight."

She smiled and went to his closet. "I better pick you out some clothes so you don't throw everything on the floor again."

"Thanks, Mom."

#

Judy opened the door, and her heart pounded indecently when she saw him. He was dressed in a navy linen suit with a red silk shirt that set off his brown eyes, and he seemed to have filled out more since she had seen him at Thanksgiving. *My God, I love this man.*

Every time she saw him, her resolve not to marry him weakened, yet she always remembered the excruciating pain his infidelity had caused her.

"I'll get my coat." She gave him a peck on the cheek and turned to the hall closet. He took her arm and gently but firmly turned her to him. Then he kissed her full on the lips, gently, but with passion.

Oh, shit. I'm lost, she thought. They went toward the car, Judy a contender for the Miss Colorado title, and George a contender for…

#

The lights twinkled on the lake as stately white swans cruised the water. It was a crisp Colorado evening, still bright enough to see Cheyenne Canyon. Broadmoor dining was exquisite, with soft tinkling sounds coming from the lounge across the foyer, delicate smells wafting from the kitchen, and the subtle movement of waiters as they served the rich and powerful.

Judy looked across the table at George. "What's on your mind, George? You sounded so desperate."

He reached across and took her hand, and she didn't pull away. "Judy, I've been offered an awful lot of money to play professional hockey for the next five years. But the party has offered me a political plan after law school that will lead me to run for president. I don't know what to do."

She looked into his chocolate eyes and watched as he brushed back the wayward forelock from his forehead. *How could he even consider professional sports, when he could become a prominent leader?*

"I can't decide for you. You have to decide what you truly want."

"I know there's a lot of prestige in the offer I got from the Avalanche. No rookie has ever received that kind of contract."

"Do you want to be president? Or does your father want you to be president?" She saw the wounded look in his eyes as she confronted him with the question he didn't want to face.

Anger was just below the surface as he dropped his eyes to the table before replying. "Cheap shot. But you may be right. I've never been able to get his approval since Matt died." He looked up with wet eyes. "Judy, he hasn't come to one game, not one, since the accident."

She squeezed his hand gently. "I know, I know. George, this conversation has to be about what you want, deep inside. This time it's not about pleasing your father. You have to want something because you want it."

"I do."

"What?"

"I want you."

She sighed and took a sip of wine to gather herself for what was coming. "What difference would it make, if—and that is a big 'if'—I said yes. How would that help you decide?"

"I would jump at law school, politics, and making a difference. I would have the grandest lady in the world at my side. My God, I could become president with you beside me."

"Well, take me out of the equation, and decide what you want, with or without me by your side."

Their dinner came, and the conversation shifted to the approaching Miss Colorado contest, the playoff games, the whirl of holiday parties, and so forth.

On the steps of the Olsons' home, they made a date for New Year's Eve. She came easily to him for a passionate kiss, and she went inside knowing they had rekindled their love.

She looked forward to New Year's Eve. They would go together. Judy was weakening.

$ $ $

CHAPTER FOURTEEN

Ronald sat in the office of Governor Benton. As usual when he came to the ranch, he was not happy. Somehow, Joe Willie had made it through three years at Harvard, and now he was due to enter his senior year. Benton had called yesterday and asked him to come to the ranch. Ronald was feeling more pressured; the success of moving the labs and the remaining Nefazians was his responsibility. Today the burden seemed unbearable. He would make it happen no matter what it took.

He sipped his drink as Benton handed him the letter on official Harvard Law School stationery. Benton looked old and tired.

"The dean of law wants to expel him?"

Ronald perused the letter, which said that if Joe Willie did not bring his grades to passing and start attending classes, the university would have no choice

125

but to ask him to leave. He put the letter on Benton's desk and went to the bar to refill his glass with Chivas, no ice.

Sipping his comfort, he spoke through clenched teeth, "Dean Ogilvy is a good Federalist member. I think a nice vacation for him and his family at the Stanley in Estes Park might be a good idea."

Benton joined him at the bar for a stiff drink. "I agree. Do you think you can convince him to let Joe Willie graduate?"

Ronald's laugh was mirthless. "If the five of us don't have enough persuasive power for that, then there's no way we can win a presidency."

He put down his glass and looked around. So much had happened in this room; they were not about to lose it all now. He brushed lint from his silk suit. He liked how he looked in green, and thought the mint shirt with a kelly green tie complimented the suit perfectly.

"I'll arrange a meeting with Dean Ogilvy this Saturday at the Baldpate Inn," Ronald said. "Be there, and you'd better plan on entertaining Dean Ogilvy and family during the Easter holiday. A sightseeing and golfing trip to Sedona is always a nice offering for Easterners." Ronald tossed down his drink and turned to leave.

"I'll see you Saturday," Benton said to Ronald's back.

#

Lillian heard the last of the conversation. She didn't know what had happened, but every time Ronald came to the ranch, it meant Joe Willie was in trouble. She walked toward the barn, slapping her straw hat against her leg and trying to clear away the fear of what might come next. She did not want Joe Willie here. Their meetings at Harvard and the ranch were unbearable. She didn't want him expelled.

She remembered their wedding. It had been hot news for Gould's papers and television for months. Shots of the happy couple traveling through Monte Carlo, France, Spain, and Switzerland had entertained the paparazzi for weeks.

Her most vivid memory of the celebrated honeymoon was the night in Monte Carlo, when Joe Willie had raped and beat on her. He did it like a professional, hitting her in places where it wouldn't show. He was drunk and ugly.

She sounded like a little girl when she called Senator Strom the next morning. "Daddy, I have to get out of this marriage. The man is an animal. He raped me."

She sobbed hysterically as she told her father about the incident. Joe Willie came to her and hung up the phone. He knelt before her with tears in his eyes and begged her to forgive him, trying his best to smile. His smirk and her hatred were all she saw and felt.

"Leave me, goddamn you. Get out." Lillian remembered how bad it had hurt her to stand. She moved away from him. "Leave now, or I'll kill you, you bastard."

Joe Willie looked hurt as he turned to leave, but at the door he stopped and gave her an evil smirk. "You're mine, for better or for worse. Ronald won't let you out of this marriage. You're a slut for Tom Lacy, but not for me. Well, so be it, but you'll never be free of me. The Power Council won't release you."

The phone rang as he left her room. It was Ronald. "Lillian, your father tells me you're having some problems. How can I help?"

She could hear an extension pick up. "Daddy, are you on?"

"Yes, listen, honey, it's going to be okay. Ronald has a solution. Hear him out."

She began crying again. "Daddy, please bring me home. I can't live with this man. Please."

"Now Lillian," Ronald said, "we all know Joe Willie can be trying, but we have an organization to take care of. The Federalists are far more important than a few rough words between a husband and a wife."

"Damn it, don't patronize me! I made a deal, and it did not include getting raped."

She could not believe she had spoken like that to Ronald. No one crossed him; everyone was afraid of him.

"Lillian, for the rest of the trip you will have separate accommodations. I'll post a guard so Joe Willie won't enter your room uninvited. All you have to do is dress nicely, smile, go to dinner, and be seen with him. Gould will cover the photo opportunities. Just do your job, and we'll keep Joe Willie out of your bed. Okay?"

"Honey, do as he says. You'll be kept safe, and it's only for four more weeks. Please, my baby girl. Do it for your Daddy."

Lillian knew she had been sold out. "Okay, but keep him away from me."

She heard her father hang up. One more time she had prostituted herself so the men in her life could gain political power.

"Thank you, Lillian, you've made a great contribution to the party," Ronald added before hanging up, too.

"Fuck you!" she said to an empty room.

#

"Hi, sweet gal, you look pretty upset," Tom said gently. "I hate to see you this way. What's up with Joe Willie?" He put his arm around Lillian's shoulder as they walked together to the barn.

"I'm afraid they're going to send him home from Harvard. He's screwing up again. Tom, I can't go through with this. Take me away."

"I can't." She heard him grit his teeth so hard, she was sure he had chipped one. "Damn it, Lillian, I'm sorry. If I was any kind of man, I'd take you out of here. But Tammy would die, because she wouldn't get her treatments. I'm a pitiful specimen of a man."

"No, you're not. I understand. I just don't want him here making demands."

"Come on, you don't know if they're sending him back here or not." He pulled her closer. "We'll ride up the canyon. You'll feel better."

Lillian stopped and stared at him. "Tom, don't be condescending. I know you can't do anything about it. Just shut up and be with me."

"I'm going to tell Benton I want my full year's salary in advance. I'll go into Sedona and set up a trust account for Tammy Jean. I could put every penney in her account, then if anything happened to me, Tammy Jean would be guaranteed treatments for some time." Lillian sensed that Tom feared trouble if Joe Willie did return.

He pulled Lillian to him and kissed her gently. "It'll be all right, Lillian. I love you."

Another man wanting her to stay with Joe Willie. Lillian felt trapped in a life she hated.

$ $ $

CHAPTER FIFTEEN

It was time to dress for his meeting with Dr. Ogilvy. Ronald came in from his hunt dreading the begging and bargaining ahead. He knew they would convince Ogilvy to give Joe Willie his degree; it was simply a matter of finding out how much money it would take.

Ronald liked their lodge, nestled in the vast green Roosevelt National Forest and the Arapaho Recreation area. They were so deep in the wilderness that it was nearly impossible for anyone to find their obscure facility. He had personally selected the site years ago when they had discovered how the thin air of the Colorado high country made cloaking their ships so easy. They could slip in and out of their lodge, landing and taking off from Trail Ridge Road and Estes Park, with neither radar nor humans ever spotting their ships.

For thirty years, they had been bringing their Generian people to the camp near the lodge for acclimation into Earth's society. No one but the Council was allowed in the lodge. It was there they could take off their skins and be Nefazians.

The Federalist Party had grown rapidly from a nucleus of Nefazians and humans recruited from the Republican Party. The recruits were given shots which produced the temperament and features of the Generian race. Most were calculating, with a single purpose: to populate Earth.

Mainstream Federalists did not know the ultimate goal was for Ronald and the Nefazians to rule Earth. Ronald poured himself a tall Scotch and enjoyed his nakedness. He chuckled as he remembered a similar hunt. He had been buck naked, deep in the woods, when he came upon a group of wilderness campers. At the first sight of him, they had run into the woods, screaming, "Bigfoot!"

"You're looking smug today." John Woods came into the room and poured himself a vodka. "I really enjoyed a couple of days up here away from the world, and I had some good hunting. How about you?"

Ronald had just gorged himself on a meal of raw deer. "I'm refreshed. I need to be, because I really hate dealing with Dean Ogilvy and his fat little family. But that's the price we pay, isn't it?"

He took a large gulp of Scotch and stretched out on one of the red leather sofas. "John, we're so close, just fourteen more years and we'll have our own president.

We'll take over Earth and be done with the stupid humans. It'll be good to move our cloning labs from Nefaz."

"Sounds good to me, but don't think we have it made," Jack Ingersol said as he joined them. Blood dribbled down his hairy chest. "There are still a lot of things that could go wrong."

Ronald could see that Jack had had a good morning hunt. "We will not fail, Jack. It's too well planned, thanks to you and the stupidity of this race." He knocked off his drink. "Joe Willie is such a puppet, if we can just keep his drinking and whoring out of Sam's papers and television."

"That is a very big if, Ronald, with a lot of pay-offs between here and the White House."

Tired of the conversation, Ronald said, "Get dressed." It was an order. He stood and stormed out of the room. Donning his human skin, he covered it with a new three-piece maroon linen suit, set off by a red shirt and a white tie.

#

Sometime around October 15th, the Baldpate Inn closed for the winter, and Ronald was glad they could get in for lunch. He liked the deck, the smell of fresh-baked breads and homemade soups mingling with the scent of pine trees. Plus, they served bona fide name-brand liquor.

He left the lodge in a white limousine to go to the Stanley Hotel in Estes Park, where he would pick up the Ogilvy family. The other Council members and Benton would meet them at the inn.

Sitting on its hilltop perch, the Stanley was an impressive establishment. White puffy clouds played in the deep blue sky behind the hotel. The only thing that marred the scene was a family of fat people standing on the front steps. Dr. Ogilvy, his wife, and his two children were all round. Ogilvy was short, with thick glasses and thin grimacing lips. Instead of being a clone, he was one of the humans who had received Generian supplements.

Ogilvy was a dependable party man, but he had a moral line concerning his law school, and today Ronald would find out how much it would cost for Ogilvy to cross that line.

Lunch was perfect, as usual, and pleasing aromas filled the room. All the men stood as Mrs. Ogilvy scuttled her round son and daughter off to the rest room. It was apparent that the eleven- and twelve-year-old children were bored with the talk, the view, and all the hundreds of keys hanging in the Key Room.

Ronald turned to Dean Ogilvy. "Why don't we send them back to the Stanley? John can drive you back in his Hummer after we finish talking."

Ogilvy's thick glasses hid his eyes so that it was hard to tell what the man was thinking. He dabbed at his thin mouth with his linen napkin and cleared his throat. "I believe we're finished here. Joe Willie is

134

not a student who should be attending Harvard Law School. I'm forced to send him back to Arizona."

Ingersol saved the day by whipping out two of his latest miniature game computers. Barely the size of a deck of cards, they were experimental and would be very pricey when they hit the Christmas market. "Dean Ogilvy, I almost forgot, I have one of these for each of the children. They're the very latest in hi-tech games, and I think they'll enjoy them."

Ronald watched as the dean accepted the proffered gifts. *Let the games begin!* he thought. He turned to Mrs. Ogilvy as she returned with the children. "Mrs. Ogilvy, would it be all right with you if we kept your husband a bit longer? The limo can take you and the children to the hotel, and we'll drive him down later."

"Of course, whatever he needs to do."

Jack gave the boy and girl the new miniature game computers, and they squealed with delight. Ronald motioned the driver to take them away. The fall air was bracing as the men went out on the deck with snifters of brandy.

"I can't thank you gentlemen enough for the vacation, the lunch, and of course the game computers. I just wish I could do something for you."

Ronald nearly choked. This meeting was too important; whatever it took, they would get Joe Willie his law degree. The idiot would never get in the Senate without it.

John Woods took his turn next. "You know, Dean Ogilvy, we have an experimental sun-powered vehicle, much like a golf cart, only this one is a luxury model. It has many features for colder areas, like where you live. Would you consider using one to get around campus this winter? It would surely help us work out the bugs, if you'd be kind enough to try it out."

"Well, that would be fun. Of course, if it will help. I want you all to know, I'm a strong Federalist and I want to do all I can for the party. But this young boy is troublesome. I can't give him any more slack."

Rollins took his turn. "You know, Dean, I was thinking of funding some research for law student software. It would be tied into the food market and the legalities of FDA regulations. You could press a button and come up with all the laws related to regulating and de-regulating. It would give some law school a real edge in placing their graduates with major corporations. Do you think your school could help us work out the glitches? Maybe try out such a program?"

Ogilvy removed his glasses and wiped them with his cocktail napkin. Ronald noted that behind those glasses were greedy little gray eyes. "That would be wonderful. I hardly know what to say. I feel terrible that I can't reciprocate in some way for your generosity."

Gould stepped to the plate. "My communications network wants to feature a top law school for a series of feature stories. Worldwide coverage and advertising dollars will go into an endowment fund for the school selected." He paused. "Should come to six, maybe eight million for the school we choose."

Ogilvy's glasses were steaming again. "My, how exciting. I have been thinking about Joe Willie. Maybe I could initiate some sort of innovative correspondence course for him, if there was a legitimate reason for him not to be on campus. Maybe a tutor in Arizona, maybe work through the University of Arizona. Some ideas are coming to me. I would really like to help if I can. If there was just some reason for him to be at home rather than on campus…"

Ronald had had all the games he could take. He wrote a number on his napkin and passed it across the table to the dean.

"What's this?"

"This is a number for a Swiss bank account. We can't offer you money for a degree, but we can give you an account number. When Joe Willie receives his law degree, my guess is that there will be funds added to that account."

Ogilvy wiped his glasses and his forehead with his now wet napkin. "Ah, how much are we talking about?"

Ronald loved it. Ogilvy's unadulterated greed was now on the table. "I believe it opened with $10,000 dollars, and upon graduation it will grow to $1,000,000."

Ogilvy swallowed hard. "I'll start work immediately on a creative extension program for Joe

Willie. Can you create a necessity for him to be in Arizona?"

Ronald stood, signaling the meeting was over. "We'll take care of it. Thank you, Dean Ogilvy."

Governor Benton, who had sat silently through the entire negotiation, now stood to shake hands with Ogilvy. "Thank you. You and your family must be our guests for Easter vacation. Sedona is lovely in the spring."

$ $ $

CHAPTER SIXTEEN

Ronald clicked on the video surveillance in the kitchen of the Benton ranch. He needed to watch Carl. Carl didn't want to do what he'd been told to do. He said doctoring and manipulating Joe Willie was one thing, but putting Janice Benton through the rigor of a simulated stroke was not something he wanted to do. Ronald had reminded him that his very existence was dependent on the Council, and that he would damn well do what he was told.

Janice Benton would never know what hit her. Ronald watched and listened. Janice was sitting at her usual breakfast spot looking out at the red sandstone wonders of their Sedona ranch.

"Good morning, Carl. You're up early."

"Morning, Mrs. Benton." Carl poured himself coffee. "Can I get you more coffee?"

"Yes, thank you."

Carl picked up her cup and took it to the coffee bar, where he poured the drug into her coffee. The serum would induce a mild stroke.

The drug was designed so that the effects of the stroke would last for a couple of years; then Janice would recover fully. It was an awful ordeal for her to go through, but nothing mattered to Ronald more than the success of their plan.

Carl watched as she sipped her coffee and stared out the window. "The coffee seems a little bitter, doesn't it?"

"No, mine is fine."

In less than two minutes, Janice Benton was on the floor turning blue, her mouth twisted by the stroke. Carl called 911 for the lifeline chopper. She would be airlifted to Phoenix.

Ronald smiled and turned off the surveillance. Now Joe Willie had a reason to leave Harvard. He would come home to be by his mother's side.

#

Lillian and Tom heard three shots, the signal to return to the ranch at once. Lillian kicked her horse and he jumped into a full gallop, with Tom's steed racing alongside. Carl was at the corral, waving frantically and still holding the rifle.

Tom jumped off his horse before it came to a full stop. "What the hell has he done?"

"It's not him," Carl explained. "Miss Janice had a stroke. She's been airlifted to Phoenix."

Lillian felt her stomach knot. She had come to love Janice, and thought of her as a second mother. Janice and Tom were the two who made life at the ranch, and her marriage to Joe Willie, bearable.

"How bad?" Tom asked.

"Bad. There's a police escort here to take you to the hospital. Drive the Porsche and go with them."

Lillian noticed the two police cruisers, their lights strobing.

She and Tom ran to the black Porsche. Tom drove, one cruiser leading them and the other following. With flashing lights and sirens blaring, they sped off to Phoenix.

When they arrived, Lillian ran down the corridor of the intensive care unit, oblivious to the antiseptic smells and the purr of life-support systems.

Governor Benton was pacing in the small waiting room. Lillian had never seen him so out of control. His pain was evident on his face. Lillian knew he and Janice loved each other. Janice had put up with the corruption in his life and had kept quiet. As much as he could, he had shielded her from the details. At this moment, he looked old and frightened.

"How is she?"

"Oh, God, Lillian, I don't know. The doctors are with her. They're not telling me anything."

He came toward her, and they held each other, sobbing quietly. Tom looked on.

"Thanks, both of you, for being here," Ronald said as he entered the waiting room.

Benton leapt at him. "You son of a bitch. What did you do to her?"

Ronald fell backward. Benton grabbed him by the lapels of his pinstriped suit and cocked his arm, fist clenched, ready to ram it into Ronald's face.

"Whoa, hold on. Stop it!" Tom jumped between them, forcing them apart. Nurses and staff stared. One of the male orderlies moved in to help Tom.

Benton was still mouthing obscenities. Lillian took his arm, trying to calm him, but he brushed her aside.

"Governor, calm down." Tom moved him toward the chapel, while the orderly pulled a surprised Ronald along, too.

#

Ronald straightened his suit and tie. *A different time and place, and I'd eat him for lunch.*

"Calm down," Tom ordered. "They'll throw us all out of here."

Benton was still red with rage, but Ronald had regained his composure. Now he had to convince the governor that the Council had had nothing to do with Janice's stroke. *Damn Carl.* He had given her too much. They didn't want her to die. If she died, Joe Willie had no reason to stay in Arizona. The plan was to portray him as the grieving, nurturing son, who stayed out of Harvard to be with his incapacitated mother.

"Bill, relax. I'm not the enemy." He reached out to pat Benton on the shoulder.

Benton shook his hand away and said in a low, angry voice, "I don't know how, but I know you did this to Janice. If she dies—"

"Bill, we had nothing to do with this. There were other plans to bring Joe Willie home. How could you think that we would do this?" He spoke gently, reassuringly.

"It's too coincidental." Benton sat down in one of the pews and put his head in his hands. "Just leave me alone."

Ronald looked at the pathetic human. *They are so emotional.* He left Benton and returned to the waiting area. Joe Willie was flying from Harvard in John's Lear to be by his mother's side.

The press was gathering in the lobby. Ronald went to make a statement for the family.

#

Two hours earlier, the phone jangled, making Joe Willie's hair stand on end. He was so hung over, his hair hurt, and the ringing sounded like a brass band marching through his brain. Joe Willie rolled over three or four bodies, male and female, trying to find the phone.

What a night! Three guys and two women. He had enjoyed the men most of all, but he had performed well with the women too. He knew his manhood image was intact.

Joe Willie's apartment was off-campus, so he was not under campus supervision, and his parties were infamous among the party crowd. Nothing was too bizarre for Joe Willie. He had never made many friends in high school, but now he was popular. He had his own place, lots of money, and his wedding vows didn't stand in the way of his hunger for booze and sex. His crowd was not known as the academic crowd.

He found the phone under a pile of jockey shorts and bras. "Hullo." His tongue felt like bear hair.

"Joe Willie, it's John Woods here."

"Jesus, John, why're you calling so early? It's only eleven." Joe Willie wandered to the kitchen away from the mound of bodies on the bed. The room smelled of booze, pot, and sex.

"Your mother had a stroke, and she may not live. I'm at the airport with the Lear. Get here ASAP."

"She what?" Joe Willie shook his head to clear it of the cobwebs made by alcohol's spider.

"She had a stroke. She's in intensive care. Pull yourself together and get here right away."

"Oh shit," Joe Willie said as John hung up. He started pulling on clothes, hoping they were his. He called a cab and washed his face, but didn't take time to shave.

Settled in the cabin of John's Lear jet, he was pouring down juice and strong black coffee. The familiar pain of the hangover began to subside. He was in shock. *Don't let her die, please.*

Joe Willie knew nothing of prayer, or God, or any of that stuff. But he knew he had depended on Janice to like him even when Benton and the Council were mad at him. If he was capable of loving any woman, she would be the one. If she died, he would have no one. Lillian didn't love him. She put up with him, but she was always humping Tom.

John entered the cabin and motioned the pretty red-headed hostess to bring him coffee. "How you doing?" he asked Joe Willie.

Joe Willie's eyes filled with tears. "I'm scared. I'm really scared. She can't die."

"She has the best doctors. They got her to the hospital quickly, and she's a fighter. She'll make it." John's voice didn't sound as confident as his words.

Joe Willie catapulted from his limousine when it pulled in front of the hospital. His strange, lumbering gorilla movements were exaggerated as he hurried to the intensive care unit.

There he saw Lillian and Tom seated on the tan couch in the waiting room. Tom had his arm around her, and she was nestled into his shoulder. Joe Willie felt his anger rise. He hated Tom Lacy.

"How is she? If you can break away from your lover long enough to give a damn." His voice was shaking with anger and fear.

Lillian came to him, looking beautiful in her tight jeans, denim shirt, and red scarf, smelling of horse, perfume, and Tom Lacy.

He felt his anger melt as she took him in his arms. He went into the comfort of her embrace, and tears poured from his blue eyes. Tom came to them and patted him on the back.

"She'll make it, Joe Willie. She will, she's a strong woman."

Joe Willie pulled Lillian closer, feeling her ample breast, her femaleness. Lillian motioned Tom away. Joe Willie smirked. He knew that tears always worked with women. He remembered his first meeting with Janice, and more tears flowed.

Benton came from the chapel just as Tom was leaving. Lillian and Joe Willie were still enclosed in a comforting hug.

"Any word?" Benton asked Tom.

"None yet. Joe Willie just got here. I'll go back to the ranch."

The doctor came into the waiting room in his green scrubs. All of them grouped around him to hear the news.

"If she lives through tonight, she has a chance. Her heart has suffered severe trauma, but she's a strong woman, so we're encouraged."

"What are her chances of making it through the night?" Benton's voice cracked as he fought back tears.

The doctor looked him in the eye. "Fair. Not good, but fair."

Joe Willie asked, "Can we see her?"

"Just your father."

Tom asked the question they all dreaded. "And if she lives? What's the prognosis?"

"She'll be paralyzed and probably will not be able to speak. But people with this degree of damage have been known to regain some speech and mobility. Let's just get her through tonight."

He patted Benton's arm and motioned him to follow. Benton turned to Tom. "You and Carl fix the downstairs guest room for her. She'll be coming home."

Joe Willie felt like the small boy who had come from Nefaz, lost and alone. He looked up as Ronald returned from the news conference.

"Any news?" Ronald asked.

Tom explained the situation as Joe Willie remained in Lillian's arms. "Fly me to the ranch," Tom said. "We have to prepare a room for her on the main floor."

As Ronald and Tom entered the elevator, Joe Willie collapsed. Lillian ran for one of the nurses. They took him to a room and gave him a sedative and a concentrated shot of B12.

$ \$ \quad \$ \quad \$ $

CHAPTER SEVENTEEN

Judy was surprised when Governor Blair asked that she come to see him. She had known him for years, but she could not remember ever having had a one-on-one conversation with him. Hilda showed her into his office. He came to her, taking her hands in his, and ushered her to one of the red leather chairs.

"What would you like to drink?" He was already sipping on a bloody mary.

"Nothing, thank you. I have to get on I-25 before traffic and the storm. I'd better not drink."

Judy looked at him with interest, wondering if George would still be so handsome when he reached his father's age.

The governor sat on the sofa to her right and reached out to pat her hand. She knew the signs; he wanted something from her.

"Judy, I understand you and George have made plans for New Year's Eve. Dare I hope the two of you are getting back together?"

"Well, I wouldn't exactly say that, Mr. Blair."

"Please, call me Matt. You're no longer a little girl." He gave her a full Blair smile. "You're practically Miss Colorado, or so I hear."

"I don't know about that. I may drop out of the contest. Never mind, what do you want?"

He sat back on the sofa, crossing his long legs, and turned toward her. "Judy, you probably know I've been a little distant from George since the accident." He took a long sip of his drink before continuing. "I've never quite recovered from the loss."

Suddenly he stood up and began pacing, almost as if he were talking aloud to himself. She watched.

"Judy, the party wants to start grooming George for a run at the presidency. He needs to pass the bar, get a couple of terms in the Senate, and then the party is willing to throw their full strength behind him. The Federalists are gaining momentum and power. We need to get them out of control, or they'll get their man in the White House."

Judy silently watched him. He quit pacing and came back to sit facing her. "Judy, these people are not just our political enemies, they're evil. We must regain dominance, and George has to get off this kick of becoming a national hockey hall-of-famer. Judy, we want you to get him on course."

She laughed and walked to the door. "Governor, I love George. I always have, and I'm sure I always will. Whether I'll be his wife or not, I don't know. That will depend on George, not you, not the party, and not any political deal."

Matthew Blair came to her and set his hand on her shoulder. "Well, that's pretty clear. Judy, please at least consider going back to him."

"I'll tell you what." Her voice was cold. "If you attend the playoff games this season, I might consider a reconciliation."

"Thank—"

"Don't thank me. I didn't say I would. I said I might. You've hurt your son with your selfishness long enough. You lost a son, but George lost his brother and his father. He deserves better. I'll decide whether to marry him or not. But I can guarantee you, if you don't start treating him like a son, you and your politics will never be a part of our lives. Treat him right, and I may help you take him to the White House."

She opened the door and left a surprised Governor Blair staring after her.

#

George was dressing for a hike into Waldo Canyon. It was a hike he often took when he needed to think, just a short drive west on Ute Pass and then into the canyon. He liked the smell of the juniper, pine, and

Grambel oaks, and he often saw bighorn sheep and deer. He was grateful to the old hunter forester, Sam Dilts, who had taken the time to lay out the Waldo Canyon Trail. Millions had enjoyed its beauty.

He saw Judy pull away from the house. Strange, what was she doing here? And why hadn't she come to talk to him? Oh well, he would see her soon, and he would have an answer for her.

He would have preferred to climb a fourteener, but the snow made it impossible, and the coach didn't allow his players mountain hiking with the playoffs this close.

George stopped to rest at the spot where he could look south toward Pike's Peak. Seven ragged mountain sheep eyed him suspiciously, but continued grazing nearby. A fine snow started to fall. He could see himself skating the Stanley Cup around the arena, maybe at the Pepsi Center, going over to kiss Judy and his strong sons. But he could also see himself walking down the staircase in the White House, formally attired and with a radiant Judy on his arm. He liked both images.

"Hey, kiddo, make up your mind. I'm freezing."

George jumped to his feet and spun around. "Damn it, Matt. Stop doing that."

He heard Matt's familiar laugh, but there was no one here but himself and the sheep. "I can stop doing this as soon as you get your head on straight."

"What do you mean?"

"Brother, I'm your spirit guide. My trips to help you are limited. George, you have to figure out who you are, who you want to be. Stop trying to be me. Stop trying to please Father."

"I'm not."

"You are. You have been since the accident." The voice faded.

"Don't go yet, Matt."

"George, you can have an impact on the world. Don't squander your gift. Your gift is not playing professional hockey. Your gift is your desire to help people. People need you."

The voice was gone, replaced by canyon silence. George was shaken by the visit from Matt. As usual, he took his brother's words to heart. *I guess I know what to do. I really want to help people. I will get active in the party. If I'm elected, I'll try to bring some civility back to Washington.*

He hurried down the trail to his car. *On New Year's Eve I'll tell Judy of my decision, then I'll ask her to take my ring. She'll be one hell of a partner, if she'll have me.*

#

It was Sunday morning of exam week, and Judy was bleary-eyed from studying. She had given the Denver Post reporter her last Miss Colorado interview on Friday afternoon. She was allowing herself the luxury of one more cup of coffee before she hit the law library. Stretching out with the *Gazette Telegraph*, she turned to the sports page, and there was George in his Colorado College Tigers uniform, smiling at her. His runaway forelock had fallen over his eyebrow.

"Sports fans will be shocked and disappointed." The article's lead line jolted her into a sitting position.

George Blair, premier right-winger for the Colorado College Tigers, announced today he will not accept the twenty-five-million dollar five-year contract offered by the Colorado Avalanche.

Blair said he has decided to finish his law degree and follow the family tradition of public service. Blair went on to say that he felt he owed a debt to his country and he wanted to spend his life trying to help those less fortunate.

Asked when he would make his first run for public office, he declined to answer, saying there was a lot of schooling between now and then. When asked who would win the playoff between the Denver University Pioneers and the Colorado College Tigers, he replied, "Grrrrr!" Hockey fans will miss his brilliant play. It is this reporter's sense that a strong Democratic leader might be emerging.

Judy reached for the phone. George's line was busy.

#

George showered and went to the kitchen for coffee. He had felt surprisingly lighthearted since he had given the interview to the Gazette reporter and talked with the coach.

The Blair kitchen always smelled of cinnamon rolls and fresh ground coffee. As usual, Hilda was humming and bustling around the stove, Martha was at the table reading the Denver Post, and both were drinking coffee. George sneaked up behind his mother and gave her a chin rub.

"George, you startled me." A smile took over her face.

"What's new? You seemed very involved with the paper."

Hilda brought his juice and coffee. Martha turned the society page around so he could see the article. Smiling out at him was a color picture of Judy in her swimsuit. The banner under the picture announced, "Contender for Miss Colorado quits for law degree."

George spilled his coffee. Both Hilda and Martha fussed around him, cleaning up his mess, while he continued to read the article.

Miss Judy Olson, thought by many to be the sure winner of this year's Miss Colorado pageant, said today she is stepping out of the contest to devote full time to passing the bar.

Miss Olson said she didn't want to let the people of Colorado down. If she had been chosen, she would not have had time to fulfill her duties, and in fairness to the other contestants she wanted to step down early.

When asked if she had a romantic interest, the beautiful Miss Olson smiled and said, 'No comment.' This reporter had a sense there might be more in her near future than passing the bar.

George jumped up, knocking over his juice this time, and ran up the stairs to his phone. Punching Judy's number on the speed dial, he waited. Her line was busy.

As soon as he hung up the phone, it rang. Whoever it was, he would get the hell off the line quickly so he could reach Judy. "Who's this?" he answered gruffly.

"Nice way to answer your phone, George."

"Judy! I've been trying to reach you. You quit—does that mean what I want it to mean? Are we getting back together?" He was breathless and could feel his heart beating in his temples, as well as other places.

"Doesn't mean anything, except I need a ticket for the Denver games."

Disappointed, he'd thought for sure she was coming back to him. "Well, you can use my father's and go with Mom."

"No, I think that seat will be taken. Get me something near your mom."

"Okay." *Damn.*

"I'll be there Friday. And George, I'm proud of your decision." She paused. "By the way, do you still have that ring you've been carrying around all these years?"

George nearly wet himself. "Oh God, yes, Judy. Yes, I do. I love you."

"I love you too, George. See you Friday."

He let out a whoop that caused both Martha and Hilda to come running to his room to see if he was all right.

#

Matthew Blair read the two Sunday papers. He picked up the intercom. "Martha, have you given away my seat for the playoff games?"

"No, but there are people who want it. Why?"

"Don't give it away. I'm going."

$ $ $

CHAPTER EIGHTEEN

George and Judy announced their engagement at the New Year's Eve ball. George was happier than he had ever remembered being. New Year's morning, as he went to the kitchen for coffee, he was dumbfounded when his father called him into his office.

He was even more surprised when his father came to him and put an arm around his shoulders. He hadn't shown any affection since the day George had told him about Evelyn being pregnant.

"George, I'm so glad you and Judy made up. When is the wedding?" He brought his bloody mary to the coffee table with a cup of coffee for George. George rarely drank since the summer with Evelyn.

His father sat on the red leather sofa and motioned George to sit across from him.

"We talked about June, a June wedding at the Broadmoor," George said. "Our church won't hold the crowd. Is that all right with you?"

"Yes, more than all right. It's perfect. I want the party leaders invited. They'll be pleased with your marriage. Now we can plan for your future."

George loathed the idea of their wedding becoming a political meeting, but he relished the look of admiration his father gave him. George would do anything to win his father's approval.

"Why is that necessary?" he asked cautiously, not wanting to anger his father.

"George, I told you some time ago that the party has plans for you. Our informants tell us the Federalists plan to skip the representative race and move their man right into the Senate for two terms, and then run him for president. We intend to match those moves. You will marry Judy, pass the bar, run for Senate, spend two terms, and then go on to the presidency."

"Um, well, that's a little fast for me. How can I be ready to run for president so soon?" He took a sip of his coffee and looked over the rim at his father.

"No, it's not too fast. If they can get their man ready, so can we. Besides, you're brighter and better looking than Joe Willie Benton."

"Joe Willie, Governor Benton's son? He's known as a womanizer and a drunk. Are you sure?"

"It doesn't matter what he is, they have the money to buy him any office. Our goal is to stop them from buying him the presidency, and you're our best prospect to defeat him."

"I don't know what to say. I…" George stood and began to pace the room.

"Say nothing. Your job is to marry Judy, pass the bar, and win your first Senate seat." He stood and came to his son, once again placing an arm around his shoulders. "I'll be attending the playoff games this year."

George felt his heart leap into his throat. He stood taller.

"Go on, get out of here. Go see Judy. I have calls to make. This is a great day for the Democratic Party."

#

The Colorado College Tigers were unbeatable. As the season closed, they overpowered each team they met in the playoffs. However, the Denver University Pioneers matched them, win for win. It looked as if it would come down to these two teams, head to head for the championship.

George and Judy were together every possible weekend. She came to Colorado Springs, or he went to Denver. They were in love, inseparable, busy with playoffs, finals, and wedding plans. George had never been happier.

Sitting in their cave, they looked out to the red sandstone colonnades which formed the Garden of the

Gods. The sun turned the formations to a deep rose color framed by Colorado blue skies.

Judy mused, "Wedding invitations are out of control. I believe your dad thinks I'm marrying the Democratic Party."

"You may be. I'm so overwhelmed with their wanting to make me president, and yet I really want to make a difference. So many things the Bush Administration put in place are really unfortunate for the country. I'd like the chance to correct those problems and make America a place for all people, not just the rich."

Judy smiled and held his hand. "I love you so much, George. You'll go down in history as a great president, and I get to be by your side. Is 'wow' a good enough word to describe our life?"

"'Wow' works for me. Hey, what about a honeymoon? Where do you want to go—England, Switzerland, France?"

"You know what I'd really like to do? I'd like to tour Colorado. Estes Park, Steamboat, Aspen, Leadville, Durango, all the towns. I'd like to hike in the back country and take pictures. I love our state. Let's spend it with the people you're going to represent."

George pulled Judy to him and kissed her long and deep. "You are amazing. I love the idea. It's perfect."

"Oops, look at the time. I have to get my butt to practice. Got to get ready for Denver University."

"Martha and I are going shopping. I'll get back-packing stuff for both of us."

They walked hand in hand toward the Blair house, enjoying the smell of spring. Aspens showed off their fuzzy buds, and the smell of pine and spruce filled the air as they too poked out new green needles.

Playoff games were scheduled Saturday and Sunday, back to back. The winner would walk away as this year's champion. George hoped his father would come. So far, he hadn't kept his promise to attend the games.

#

Colorado College won Saturday's game, 1 to 0. Denver would come out tough today. George was up early for a morning skate and team meeting. He was disappointed his father hadn't attended the game, as promised, but he hadn't really thought he would come. George found Martha and Hilda in their usual places, drinking coffee and gossiping.

"Good morning, George." Martha's face lit up when she saw George.

He took the cup Hilda handed him as he went to join his mother.

"Morning, ladies, and who are you roasting this morning?"

Hilda tittered and Martha gave him a playful swat. "You're incorrigible."

"George, I have some great news." Martha's eyes reflected her joy. "Your father is coming to the game today."

George knew his father had said he would come, and he played along with Martha. "You're kidding. He's never been to one of my games since... I mean, really?"

George knew his father wouldn't be there. He had heard it too many times before. He wouldn't get his hopes up, and then he wouldn't be disappointed.

"Really, he is coming, George." Martha looked so pleased, he leaned over and kissed her cheek.

George would never know that Judy had reminded Governor Blair of their conversation. She had insisted he take an interest in George if he wanted her help to put his son in the White House. He could start by attending George's last game.

#

When Judy entered the World Arena, it was rocking and rolling with the din of wild hockey fans, old and young alike. Both sides were trying to out-shout and out-stomp the other. The rivalry between Denver University and Colorado College was unparalleled in its intensity. At one time, in the 1950's, games had been suspended because of the fierce fighting.

Judy felt the excitement build as both teams took the ice for warm-ups and the crowd noise swelled.

Judy could hardly hear Martha as she practically shouted in her ear. "I think your future husband is the most handsome of all of them."

"Me too, but we might be a little partial," Judy shouted back. Governor Benton joined them. He sat between them and gave Judy a conspiratorial wink. "I kept my end of the deal."

"Don't worry, I'll keep my word."

She saw George look up and wave. She knew he would be ecstatic to finally have his father attending one of his games.

First period began rough and fast. George had been held in check, because he was double-teamed every time he got the puck. Judy winced each time he was driven into the boards. Twice he was hit with a high stick; always the referee was looking elsewhere. She hoped he could make it through this game without an injury. She was glad this would be his last hockey game.

George got only two shots on goal. He was the top scorer for Colorado College, and in the final minute of the first period, Denver University scored a goal. The game didn't look good for Colorado College unless they could get George free to score.

Matthew turned to Judy. "He is good, isn't he?"

"Yes, he's good, and you need to tell him you think so."

"Judy, I'm here. That should tell him."

"No, he needs to hear the words from you."

Then the crowd erupted, and further conversation was impossible.

During the second period, Judy watched as George skated with new vigor. He was able to get free several times and got several quality shots on the Denver goalie. She thought someone must have talked to the referees, because they were calling the game much tighter. George stole the puck on a turnover at the blue line and got a slap shot past the goalie. The score was now 1-1.

Judy screamed so loud, she knew she would have a sore throat the next day. Matthew stood and shouted, "That's my son."

The rest of the second period was a defensive battle up and down the ice, with neither team able to score. Neither team wanted to make a mistake that would lead to a goal for the other. With just two minutes to go in the second period, Denver University got a power play and scored another goal. They went to the locker room 2-1. Judy hoped that wouldn't hold up through the third period. She also hoped George would not be injured in the last period of play. Two players had already been taken to the locker room and hadn't returned. It had been a fierce game so far.

Third period was a real defensive battle, and Judy watched the clock, wanting it to end. With twenty seconds left in the third period, George drove toward the net past everyone for a sure goal, when the Denver defense man tripped him. George went sliding into the boards. Judy felt her heart come up to her throat.

He remained still for an instant too long. Then, slowly, he got up. He was shaken, but all right. The crowd roared. He was given a penalty shot. Judy stood with everyone else in the World Arena. George sped toward the goalie, feinting left, then right, then left at the final instant. He pulled the goalie off position and scored. The score was 2-2, and it looked like they were going to play overtime. With just fifteen seconds remaining in the third period, the game was fast, hard hockey.

Judy and Martha held hands across Matthew's lap. Five seconds to go, and it looked like overtime. With two seconds on the clock, George stole the puck. He drove the net with his superior puck handling, and sent two of the Denver players falling on the ice. At the red line, he let the puck rip with a mighty slap shot, and it hit the back of the net. Colorado College players swarmed all over him; hats covered the ice. George had not only won the game, but he had a hat trick to finish his career. The arena broke into pandemonium.

The home crowd was on its feet, screaming and clapping. Among those clapping and yelling, the loudest was Governor Blair. The teams lined up for the traditional handshake, and the Tigers did a victory lap before skating to the locker room. The crowd was still on its feet when Governor Blair collapsed and fell over the seats in front of him.

Judy and Martha screamed. "Call 911!"

#

While Martha rode in the ambulance with her husband, Judy burst into the locker room, shouting for George. Startled players just coming out of the showers grabbed towels to cover themselves.

"Get dressed," Judy said when she spotted George. "Your dad is on his way to the hospital. He collapsed."

George stared at her but didn't move, and Judy realized he was too shocked to comprehend what she was saying. Players were still scrambling to cover themselves.

"George, get dressed," she repeated.

One of his teammates came over and led George to his locker, where he helped George dress.

The parking lot was full of excited fans blowing car horns and yelling.

"What happened?" George asked as his shock lifted.

Judy pushed George into the passenger seat of her car and then entered the fray to get out of the parking area.

"Is he all right?"

"I don't know. He was unconscious. They took him to Penrose, and your mother's with him."

#

By the time they reached the hospital, George had come out of his shock. He found Martha in the emergency care waiting room. She was crying softly into his shoulder when the doctor entered.

"Mrs. Blair?"

Martha turned, tightly gripping George's hand. "I'm Mrs. Blair."

"We need to do an MRI. We've called your doctor and a brain surgeon from Denver, and they're on the way. The surgeon told us to do the test right away. Do you agree?"

George stepped forward, taking control. "Do it. Do it right now. You save him, hear me?"

During the next five hours of waiting, Judy and George took turns assuring Martha everything was fine. When he wasn't comforting his mother, George paced, musing over the situation. *Every time I get close to my father, every damn time he shows me any affection, something awful happens. I think I'm cursed.*

"Yeah, sure. Get a grip. Quit thinking about yourself. Step up to the plate. You're the Blair man in charge now."

He recognized Matt's voice immediately. "Why are you here?" He spoke under his breath, lest Judy and Martha think he'd flipped out.

"Because I may have to take him with me. It's going to be nip and tuck for a while. He may not make it. You need to be ready to be the man for this family." Matt's voice was already fading.

"Matt, wait."

167

Their family doctor entered the surgery waiting room and rubbed a hand over his tired face. "Martha, George, he has a brain tumor."

Martha gasped and collapsed on the green couch. Judy put her arms around her. George clenched his jaw and stood rooted to the spot.

The doctor turned to address George in particular. "We have to operate right away. The tumor is causing tremendous pressure on his brain, but it's small, and we should be able to get all of it easily."

"And what if you don't operate?" George asked, his voice controlled.

"He'll die."

"If you operate?"

"Eighty percent chance we'll get it, all of it, and he'll be fine. There's always a risk involved, but he should make a full recovery with no ill effects."

Martha came and stood beside George, and he put his arm around her shoulder and pulled her close.

"Then do it," George said.

Martha nodded her agreement.

They sat for another eight hours before the doctor came. "The surgery went fine. There's no malignancy, and we believe we got it all. He's going to be fine."

Relieved, Judy, Martha, and George cried together. George and Martha went to see him. He wasn't out of recovery, but the doctor let them peek in.

The doctor shook George's hand. "Go on home, get some sleep. He'll come around about noon. Come back then."

George had stepped into his role as man of the Blair family, but he still wanted his father's love and approval.

$ $ $

CHAPTER NINETEEN

Governor Blair recovered quickly and showed no ill effects from the tumor removal. George and Judy decided to proceed with their June wedding at the Broadmoor. It was attended by every dignitary of the Democratic Party.

George was on his way to the hotel when his father called him into his study. He stood and came to greet his son. George put out his hand in greeting and was taken aback when his father pulled him into a warm embrace.

"George, this is a big day for you and for the party. I have a little something for you. Come outside with me."

George followed, still warmed by the embrace, though it had been brief. It made him feel good. Now he was curious. What was his father up to?

They walked down the tiled entry toward the front door, and he heard Hilda and Martha giggling and running out the kitchen door. Governor Blair flung open the front door, and there in the driveway, complete with red ribbons, was a brand new forest-green Land Rover.

"Whoa!" George turned toward his father, who held out a set of keys. Martha and Hilda came running up to hug him.

"Do you like it?" Martha chirped.

"What's not to like? Wait till Judy sees it. Thanks, Dad."

"You deserve it, son, you deserve it. Now get on down to the hotel. You don't want to be late for your wedding, do you?"

George felt as if he'd just won first prize in the favorite son contest. He knew his dad could never tell him he was proud, but his gift tried to say it for him.

He hugged all of them and ran to tear off the ribbon. Jumping in his new Rover, he drove off to marry Judy. Matthew, Martha, and Hilda followed in the limousine.

#

As soon as George passed the bar, he would run for the Senate seat. Publicity was already in place, planting his name in the minds of Coloradans. The honeymoon was part of the campaign. Even though

George had objected strenuously to that plan, he had acquiesced to the leaders of the party.

George had arranged the itinerary. The first three nights were spent at the historic Stanley Hotel in Estes Park. They hiked in Rocky Mountain National Park, enjoying the raw beauty of the mountains. They hiked among deer and elk and listened to the honking of exquisite snow geese. Judy took rolls and rolls of film, mostly of George.

One evening they dined at the Baldpate Inn, oblivious to the five businessmen convened at the far end of the deck. Ronald glared at them. "Damn, they are a good-looking couple. All we have is one half of a good-looking couple. Staying here in Colorado for the honeymoon, that was a stroke of publicity genius. I think we need to stop the presses." He took a generous sip of his Scotch.

"They'll travel over the million-dollar highway, out of Ouray," John Woods said. "I hear it's a dangerous ride. Could get caught in a rock slide or something."

It would not be unusual for an accident to occur on the harrowing highway. "Great idea. Do you have their schedule tight enough to plan something?"

John smirked. "I have their schedule and a back-up plan. It doesn't have to be a rock slide."

"Well, handle it then. They're killing us with their folksy little honeymoon."

#

Judy and George drove over scenic Trail Ridge Road, spent the next two nights in Grand Lake, then moved on to Steamboat Springs. By day they hiked, picnicking in the gorgeous back county of the Colorado Rockies, and at night they dined out, meeting local people. Alone in their room each night, they learned about each other, growing more in love as they discovered the touches that gave each of them pleasure.

George got up before Judy and ordered coffee, juice, and toast. He took a quick shower, then sat on the bed caressing her face. She turned and opened her eyes.

"Good morning, Mrs. Blair. I love you."

"Mmmm, me too." She turned over, and he kissed her gently, then more passionately.

A knock on the door interrupted their foreplay. "Room service."

They sat at a small wrought-iron table on the balcony of their suite, enjoying the view while they sipped coffee and juice. George was dressed in his briefs and Judy in his plaid shirt.

"Do you want children, George?" Judy asked.

"Hundreds of them."

"Well, I'm thinking two. You can carry the other 98. I want to practice probate law."

He took her hand and smiled. "Two will be just right. So, you want to work?"

"Yes, I'm good at what I do. Alvin, your father's partner, offered me a position at their firm on Tejon. I can work into a partnership with them. I'd like to take him up on his offer."

"Do it then. I'm going right into the Senate campaign. Senator Hadley is retiring. No one knows it yet, but he'll endorse me, and I guess that makes me a shoo-in."

"Well, Senator Blair, I need to get ready for our drive. Will we go all the way to Durango today?"

"No, I thought we'd stay one night in Ouray. We can hike to the falls and enjoy the village shops. It's a fun town."

"Sounds good to me. I'm taking a shower." She bent to kiss him, and he pulled her to her feet while their lips remained locked.

He pulled free long enough to whisper, "I don't think I got clean enough. I need another shower."

#

They left Ouray early in the morning and climbed up the million-dollar highway. George drove while Judy leaned close to him. Even for native Coloradans, the highway was exhilarating.

Leaving Red Mountain, with two more hills to go before Silverton, George was hugging the center line, staying away from the drop to their right. A gray Hummer suddenly came toward them, driving too fast and crossing dangerously over the double yellow line. George swerved to avoid a head-on collision, and the Land Rover caught dirt. End over end, it plummeted to the bottom of the steep hill. The Hummer continued on without stopping.

The Rover lay driver side up on the rocky ground. George looked at Judy, who was unconscious but breathing. He could detect her pulse, but it was weak. He checked himself; just minor cuts and bleeding. *Jesus, what to do?* He knew he could crawl out, but how was he going to get Judy out? He had no idea how badly she was hurt. Blood covered her face, and her breathing was shallow.

George pulled himself out and dropped to the ground. Fog was rolling down from the high peaks. They were in a gully, not visible from the highway above.

How will they ever find us? Remembering his cellphone, George climbed back up on the Rover and reached for his backpack. Judy moaned.

"Judy, Judy, hang in there, sweetheart. I'll do something."

He felt the Rover move under him, and looking around, he realized it was resting on a small hill. Maybe he could get above it and push it upright, and then he could get Judy out. As he grabbed the backpack and jumped to the ground, the Rover swayed slightly. He jabbed 911 into the phone. No answer. He tried again and again, and then looked at the fog-covered peaks and realized there was no way a signal could reach him. He could hear Judy moaning.

He climbed the hill behind the Rover, placed both feet against the roof, and pushed with his legs—once, twice, three times. He had it rocking, and on the fourth push the Rover sat up on its wheels. He rushed to Judy's door. Miraculously, he could open it.

"Judy, can you hear me?"

"My stomach hurts. Oh God, it hurts." She moaned and slipped back into unconsciousness.

Afraid to move her but afraid not to, he made a decision. He had to get her out and cover her before she went into shock.

Gently he pulled her from the Rover and laid her on the ground. He covered her with jackets, blankets and coats, everything he could find to keep her warm. He knelt beside her. "Judy, don't you dare die." He allowed himself to cry as her eyelids fluttered.

"Judy, don't die."

Weakly, she said, "George, get help. I'm hurt bad. Get help."

They couldn't be seen where they were, and with the fog, a flare would do no good. *Shit, I don't want to leave her, but I need to set a flare on the road.*

"You go set the flare. I'll watch her." Matt's voice rang out loud and clear.

"Matt, ghosts can't watch her. I won't leave her."

"You'd be surprised what ghosts can do. Now go set a flare on the road, or I'll be taking her back with me."

"I'll be right back. Matt's watching you." After giving her a quick kiss, George grabbed the flares and scrambled to the road. As he lit the flares, he noticed that the fog was growing denser. The Rover was close enough for him to run back to the road if someone stopped. As he turned to go, he heard a car approaching, and for a second he thought it might be the Hummer coming back to see if they were dead. *No, it's something with a smaller engine.*

An old red pickup sputtered to a stop, and two men got out. One drew a pistol from his jacket as they approached. George realized his own face was covered with blood and his clothes were torn. He probably looked threatening.

"We had a wreck," he said, nearly hysterical. "Some idiot driving a gray Hummer forced us off the road. My wife needs help. She's hurt bad."

The man put his gun back in his jacket, and they followed George to the Rover. Judy was moaning softly and calling, "George, George, where are you? George, help me."

One of the men said, "I'll go back to Silverton. I can call from there." He turned to George. "You don't look so good either. Ray, stay with them, I'll get help."

As the man ran for his truck, George collapsed.

#

George woke up in the hospital in Grand Junction. His head was pounding, and his right arm was in a sling. Martha was holding his left hand. "Good, you're awake."

"What happened? I must have passed out. Where's Judy? Is she okay?"

"Easy, she's alive. She had a lot of internal bleeding and she's in intensive care."

George swung his legs over the side of the bed and attempted to get up. The room spun around him.

"Here, let's ride in this nice chair," said a blonde candy striper who helped him into a wheelchair. Martha pushed the chair toward Judy's room.

"Are you awake?" he said softly, taking Judy's hand.

She turned her head and opened her eyes. She was black and blue, and her face was swollen. Her normally deep blue eyes were misted over with pain.

"I'm awake. I feel weak. Are you all right?"

A doctor entered the room. "She's a strong woman, Mr. Blair. Lost a lot of blood, but she'll be fine."

"100%?"

"Almost. Her uterus was damaged, but I think it'll mend. Only time will tell. She may have difficulty with any pregnancies."

George's eyes filled with tears, and he held tightly to her hand. "What exactly are you saying?"

"She may do just fine, but it also may be difficult for her to bear children."

Judy began to cry. George stood unsteadily and leaned over to hold her. "We'll be together, Mrs. Blair. There's nothing we can't conquer together."

"George, Matt was there with me. I thought I was dead."

She closed her eyes and slept.

#

Once again, Ronald and the Council were lunching at the Baldpate Inn. Two years had passed since the accident, and autumn was in the air, crisp and invigorating.

"John, what did you ever do with the Hummer?" asked Ronald.

"Not to worry. It went to my auto salvage yard, where it was flattened and melted into new steel. No one will ever link us to the Blairs' terrible wreck." He smiled.

"Lot of good it did us. They got more favorable press and sympathy than they were getting on their honeymoon. Too bad they didn't die." Richard Rollins was angry. Ronald knew Richard hadn't found any fresh meat on his morning hunt, and he was irritable.

The plan was in full gear. Joe Willie had managed to get his law degree, and was now assured a Senate seat. They just had to decide how to keep him under control while he served his term. And that made Ronald nervous. "Jack, what do you have planned to keep our boy in line while he's in Washington?"

"I have a place for him in Alexandria. Carl will live with him as soon as the two of you get back from

Nefaz. Hopefully people won't start thinking he's gay."

Samuel jumped onto a solution. "That's what Lillian is for. We'll make sure she's in Washington one or two times a month. She can accompany him to all the functions. She always creates good press, especially with all that charity work. She's the best public relations tool we have."

"That's what I had planned," Jack snapped.

Ronald watched his Council members. They were all testy as the pressure built to make their plan work. Soon they could begin bringing the Nefazians to Earth. They would inhabit the world with their Generian race, while the rest of the world became their slaves. Ronald had decided to start the process of moving the cloning lab to Earth. They could hide it deep in the forest near the lodge.

#

George and Judy had both recovered from their accident. They finished law school, passed the bar, and settled into their new home in the Broadmoor. George liked the house they had found. It was close to his parents, yet they were able to maintain a private life.

He'd had a good day making campaign plans with the Democratic leaders. Soon Senator Hadley would announce his retirement and immediately endorse George to replace him in the Senate. George knew his popularity had grown because of the publicity of the honeymoon and the wreck. By now, he and Judy had endeared themselves to all Coloradans.

#

They sat in Matthew and Martha's game room, watching the results on the big screen. By eight o'clock, it was over. George had won his Senate seat by a landslide.

George was exuberant as he hugged Judy and Martha. His father gave him a firm handshake and a backslap, but no words of pride or encouragement. George ached to hear those words just once from his father: "I'm proud of you, son."

Judy was tugging on him. "Come on, we have to get down to the hotel so you can make your acceptance speech. George, I love you. I'm so proud." She kissed him and helped him with his suit coat.

#

"How did I sound?" George asked. They lay in their bed, spent from impassioned sex.

"Never better, Senator. Never better." Judy lay next to him, enjoying his smell. "I wish I was going to live with you in Washington."

George turned to look at her. "You still can. I'd love it."

"No, I need to build my fledgling practice, and I'm on several committees for social reform. No, it's best I stay here. I'll come out once a month, or you can fly home."

He lay back, sighing. "Yeah, I suppose you're right. We're now responsible adults, aren't we?"

"More than you know. The other reason I want to be here is to be close to Dr. Flynn."

"Mmmm." George was beginning to drift off. "Dr. Flynn is the obstetrician, isn't he?"

"Yes. George, I'm pregnant."

George tried to jump to his feet, but he was tangled in the silk sheets and ended up on the floor beside the bed.

Judy leaned over. "Way to go, Daddy." She was leaning over the side of the bed, laughing. He reached up and pulled her over on top of him. They rolled around in the sheets, laughing and crying.

Finally George asked her seriously, "Judy, will you be okay? Does the doctor think you can have a baby with no complications? Remember what they said after the wreck."

"He said he'll monitor me closely. That's why I need to be here. Oh God, George, I want your baby."

He held her close and vowed to tell his children every day that he loved them and was proud of them.

$ $ $

CHAPTER TWENTY

Life had passed smoothly on the Benton ranch. Joe Willie's assignments came from Harvard, Benton and Ronald did his homework, and it was graded at the University of Arizona. Gould's papers and television news kept the good son image alive. The state of Arizona came to love the son who was so dedicated to his mother that he had given up college at Harvard. A powerful women's group formed in support of him. Willie's Women, they called themselves.

It was Lillian who took care of Janice, taking her for wheelchair rides, feeding her, and reading to her. Joe Willie often joined them for reading time; it was his time with the two significant women in his life. He knew Lillian often went to Tom's cabin, but she was discreet. He had tried several times to come to her, but she had refused him.

Joe Willie was being introduced to all the right people in a series of fund-raisers, party planning sessions, and photo opportunities. Lillian was always with him, dressed to the nines, the perfect wife. Carl had cut back on Joe Willie's serums, and it turned out he was calmer without so many drugs in his system. Joe Willie enjoyed the limelight, but his favorite thrill was riding Studder along the creek bed into the red canyons, with Devil Dog running along side.

Today they stopped at the top of the canyon, where Devil Dog chased lizards and Studder nibbled on yucca blossoms. Joe Willie drank from his silver flask.

"You know something, Studder, I'm beginning to like dressing up and meeting people. As long as Carl balances my shots, I talk pretty good. They say I'm going to be president one day. Won't that be something?"

Studder snorted and pawed the ground. Devil Dog ran back to Joe Willie, panting and drooling. Joe Willie couldn't remember if this was Devil Dog number two or number three. Every time one died, Janice brought home a new one. Absentmindedly, Joe Willie stroked the soft black head and swigged on his flask.

"I really am going to be good. I'm going to quit drinking. I told Janice I would."

Janice had nearly recovered her speech, although she still slurred her words and spoke slowly. The doctors said it was a miracle that she was able to walk with a cane. Joe Willie had promised her he would quit drinking and be a good husband and son.

"I really would like to be what they want me to be. I just don't know how." He stood up, gazing out at the red stone formations.

After draining his flask, he mounted Studder and whistled for Devil Dog. Joe Willie was full of resolve to stay sober.

As he returned to the barn, he caught Lillian kissing Tom, and anger raced through his body. He began weeping as he unsaddled Studder. Running to his red Dodge, he gunned the engine, spewing gravel and red dust behind him, and sped down the road to Sedona. Gone was his resolve to stay sober. He got drunk in Cottonwood and tore up the cowboy bar.

The sheriff brought him to the ranch, and Carl called Ronald. Furious, Ronald brought two gunmen with him. They grabbed Joe Willie as he swayed drunkenly on the front stairs and dragged him toward the barn.

"I told you the last time," Ronald yelled, "if you got drunk again and risked this election, I would kill that damn stallion of yours, and that's what I'm going to do."

Sobering quickly, Joe Willie pulled out of the grasp of the two burly men. His voice rose to a hysterical pitch. "No, don't kill him. I'll never drink again, I promise. Please don't!"

The two seized him from behind by both arms, and, since they were so much taller, they carried him to the corral.

Studder was prancing and snorting, his eyes wide; he seemed to sense trouble. Usually he ran to greet Joe Willie, but now he reared and ran to the far side of the corral. He pawed at the ground and shook his magnificent head. The shooter took aim. A rifle crack and Joe Willie's scream pierced the air at the same time. Studder fell to the ground. He never knew what hit him.

Joe Willie collapsed in a heap, weeping and howling.

Jerking him to his feet, Ronald was in his face. "Devil Dog is next, then your mother if I hear even a rumor of your drinking until after the election."

Joe Willie threw back his head and wailed. Ronald let him go, and Joe Willie crumpled like a rag doll.

Ronald and his men left Joe Willie and returned to the helicopter. The Council would have a lot of spin work to do to cover up this mess. At least the police had agreed not to file charges of drunk driving and disturbing the peace. It had only cost the Council fifty thousand.

#

Tom ran from his cabin, unbuttoned shirt flying as he ran to Studder. Lillian ran too, buttoning her blouse as she went. Tom looked in disgust at the pile that was Joe Willie.

They checked Studder. He was dead. Lillian could see the anger boiling in Tom's veins. The cords on his neck stood out.

He rolled a cigarette as he looked at the stallion. "Lillian, I've had it. I'm going public. This is the last straw." He crushed his cigarette with his boot and walked toward his cabin.

Lillian grabbed his arm. "No, Tom, don't."

"I have notes, pictures, and papers. The press will pay big money for the information I have, enough for at least twenty years of treatments for Tammy. Ronald will try to kill me, but I can't condone the Federalists' conduct anymore.

Lillian ran to the main house, hoping to stop Benton from calling Ronald.

Tom threw the information in his blue truck. He stopped at the main house to say good-bye to Lillian.

Benton saw the blue truck roar to a stop in front of the house, and he stepped outside. "Now, Tom, relax. Don't do something foolish."

"I've watched for years. I've cleaned up that little shit's fuck-ups. No more, Bill. No more."

"Come on, Tom, let me add a little something to this week's check."

Tom clenched his fist so hard his nails cut into his palm. Lillian flew down the steps toward the truck. She thought Tom was going to hit Benton. She had never seen him lose control.

"Not a chance. I'm out of here." Tom jumped in the truck and gunned the engine.

Lillian ran toward the truck. "Wait Tom, I'm coming with you!"

"No. They'll kill me. I don't want you with me."

Tears flooded her cheeks. "I don't care. Tom, I love you. Take me with you."

Then the helicopter blades churned overhead, sounding trouble. Lillian knew Benton had called Ronald. Tom pulled Lillian to him for a last kiss, and then floored the gas pedal of his blue pickup. Lillian screamed.

William Benton looked after the truck. "Lillian, I'm sorry. I liked Tom, but he was going to the press. The Federalists can't cover up everything Tom can offer the tabloids."

The chopper came lower as if to land, and Benton motioned them in the direction of the truck.

"You son of a bitch." Lillian spat in the dirt near his feet and turned to enter the house.

Janice Benton watched everything and felt sick to her stomach. *What a price we all pay to stay in power.*

#

Tom knew he was a dead man, but he floor-boarded his Chevy anyway. Dust churned behind him as he left the pavement, taking the shortcut to Sedona. If he could get to the newspaper before they killed him, he'd be lucky. He had wanted to bring Lillian with him, but he refused to be responsible for her death. He hoped that, because she had stayed, they wouldn't kill her.

Fighting the wheel with one hand, he tried to roll a cigarette with the other. The road was not built for speed, and the ruts pounded his truck. He bounced around in the cab, loose dirt causing him to fishtail around the curves. Tom knew that either the road or the helicopter behind him was going to end his life.

For a few moments, clouds of dust kept the sniper from getting a clean shot at the blue truck as he leaned out of the chopper.

Tom was in a race with death, and he was losing. One shot blew out a rear tire. He fought to gain control, but he hit loose gravel and spun out, rolling end over end in the red dirt.

A second shot hit the gas tank, and the engine exploded. Fortunately, Tom was unconscious when fire consumed his truck and his evidence.

#

Six months had passed since they had killed Tom—six empty, vacant months. Sitting in her room at the ranch, Lillian thought her emotional pain would never cease. She wondered if she would ever feel alive again.

Lillian could still see him. She loved how he had worn his jet black hair slicked back, except for a runaway wave which kept falling over his left brow.

His slate blue eyes gazed back at her as she stared at the photo she carried in her wallet. The square jaw emphasized his full lips, and she ached to feel them on hers. She could almost hear his gentle voice, which had rendered her helpless when he sang love songs and strummed his old guitar.

She smiled thinking of the nights they had spent in his log cabin. Sneaking there had been so easy. She remembered how he had rolled a cigarette one-handedly in a breeze while riding his horse.

Lillian held his photo to her chest and cried a deep cry of absolute grief. She gave in to the totality of her sorrow, accepting that her loss was permanent. He was gone forever.

She went about her duties, hosting dinner parties, attending meetings, and making visits to the politically correct institutions, always dressed impeccably with her black hair perfectly in place. She no longer pulled on her jeans and blue denim shirt to go for a ride. She no longer went for rides. After the day they had killed Tom and Studder, she couldn't look in the direction of the corral or Tom's cabin.

Lillian was an empty soul moving around in a human skin, without human emotion. She kept up outward appearances, and only when alone at night did she allow herself to mourn her lover. Every night the pain came, followed by tears and quiet sobbing.

Lillian wished she had gone with him, and then she would be dead. But she had not been so lucky.

There was not enough emotion left for her to hate where she was. Her light had gone out, and she lived in the dark shadows of grief.

$ $ $

CHAPTER TWENTY-ONE

Ronald came in from his hunt. He had found only a rabbit today, but it had taken care of his craving for warm blood. His comrades were also out of costume, sitting around naked and comfortable.

"It's about time to become human again. Tomorrow is election day. We'll need to monitor the results." Jack Ingersol paced with his drink as he spoke. "Joe Willie will soon be Senator Benton."

"Jack, you're such a worrier. The fix is in. Why are you in such a hurry to slip into your skin?" Ronald knew they didn't like the full body skin each of them had to wear in the human world. He didn't mind it much since Avery had improved on it. Now the skin breathed and wasn't so unbearably hot. Ronald thought it felt like human skin, and, to be honest, he was beginning to prefer it to his own hairy pelt.

John Woods came from his hunt and poured himself a tall glass of juice. "I got most of the oil people away from the Republicans. Should be a walk in the park tomorrow for Joe Willie."

"Polls give him a big lead over his opponent," Jack said confidently. "We can hack into the system if necessary and alter results."

"We shouldn't need to. His cheerleaders, Willie's Women, really went for him. Ever since he came home, he's had the mothers' votes. Great play you gave that story, Sam." Ronald seldom praised the Council for their hard work, but today they deserved it.

Carl would also get a little bonus for the new formulas that had made Joe Willie get through ten-minute speeches, look pleasant for photo opportunities, and show the public that he was a caring person. It helped that his opponent was rumored to have skimmed money from Arizona's welfare budget.

"Let's get dressed. The chopper is waiting to take us to Scottsdale for a victory party." Ronald started pulling the skin suit over his hairy body. In moments he would look the part of a distinguished businessman, chairman of the largest biotech research lab on Earth.

#

On the morning of election day, Arizona sun filled the breakfast room with warmth and a rosy glow. Not many members of the Benton household were up at

5:00 a.m. Lillian noted the look of surprise on her mother-in-law's face when she entered the room.

"Good morning," Janice said, smiling brightly. She had nearly recovered from her stroke. Her speech was good, and she walked with a slight limp but no cane. Her doctors were amazed at her recovery.

Lillian was aware of how lonely it was for Janice. She kept to herself, except for her political duties. Lillian also knew she was becoming more like Janice every day, another beautiful trophy for an ambitious husband—except that Joe Willie was not self-driven. He was told what to do, and he did it. She doubted that Joe Willie had any ambition beyond his next sexual conquest.

"You're looking good this morning, Janice." Lillian tried to sound cheerful, though she wasn't sure she remembered how. The ache of losing Tom was with her constantly.

She poured coffee from the silver carafe and sat next to Janice. Both women looked out on the rising sun that was painting the stone formations cayenne-pepper red.

"I love mornings. I come here every day and wonder about all the what-ifs in my life."

Surprised that Janice was opening up her personal feelings, Lillian responded without thinking. "Yes, I sometimes wonder myself if I should have gone with Tom." It was no secret that Lillian had loved Tom. She just never talked about it.

"You'd be dead," Janice said matter-of-factly.

"Janice, where did Joe Willie come from?" Lillian was surprised to hear herself ask the question. She and Janice rarely spoke of their feelings. They made conversation about the next political event, what to wear, what to have the cooks prepare, and so forth. The unwritten law between them was not to get personal with one another.

"What do you mean? He was an orphan. Ronald brought him to us, and we adopted him."

"I mean, in what state was he born? I know nothing about his past. He lived somewhere until he was five. I was just wondering where he was before he came to you."

"I haven't a clue—I never cared. He was supposed to fill the void left by losing my baby, and he never did. He was a hard child to love. Sometimes I found him charming, but mostly he was self-absorbed and… strange." She smiled at Lillian and got up to pour more coffee. "I'm glad we're talking. I get so lonely."

"Political life doesn't contribute to great friendships, does it?" Now she really was curious about Joe Willie's origins. She decided to hire someone to dig up the truth about where he had been born.

#

Joe Willie was dressing for his victory speech in the suite at the Marriott Camelback Inn in Scottsdale. They always reserved a suite so Lillian would have her

195

own bedroom. Joe Willie couldn't remember the last time they'd had sex. He'd given up trying. No matter, there were plenty of women now, and whores offered themselves to him for free. Once in a while he could find a consenting male, and then he really enjoyed himself.

"Lillian, help me with these damned cuff links."

She walked into his room, stunning in the green silk dress that hung on every curve of her body. The neck was low enough to tease around her cleavage without showing it. The men would go wild tonight. It wouldn't matter if Joe Willie flubbed his speech; they would all be looking at her.

"Well, Joe Willie, how does it feel to be a United States Senator?" Her emerald eyes mocked him.

"Uh, okay, I guess," he stammered.

She had finished with one cuff link when Carl knocked softly and came in with a tray holding a small bottle of pink fluid and a syringe. "Leave the other one," he said to Lillian. "He needs a shot. I'll finish."

"Fine. Good luck with your speech tonight," she said over her shoulder as she left the room.

"Isn't she gorgeous?" Joe Willie looked longingly after her.

"Yes, sir. Now roll up your sleeve so I can give you your shot. I'm going to play a tape for you. You know the routine. Listen carefully, and the words will be fixed in your mind, and you'll be able to recite them for your acceptance speech. It's short, about five minutes." As he spoke, he emptied the syringe into

Joe Willie's arm. "Don't think, just listen. The drug will help you remember the words."

Joe Willie sat back on the couch and listened to the tape. The shots had become more and more frequent now that he was campaigning, and he hated them all the more. He could barely remember when he had last had a thought of his own. His days were nothing but a series of shots, speeches, travel, shots, speeches, and travel. He drifted off as the words of the speech scrolled through his mind.

An hour later, he and Lillian entered the ballroom to cheers and a cascade of balloons. The band played something raucous. Drums rolled, the brass section blared, and the crowd clapped and cheered. Lillian hung back as Joe Willie approached the podium, smirking at the crowd.

He held his hands up to quiet the crowd, and they clapped harder. His opponent had just finished his concession speech, and Joe Willie's supporters were crazed with the taste of victory. Eventually they quieted.

For almost a full minute, nothing came out of Joe Willie's mouth as he stared at the back wall. The room grew silent as the crowd waited. Several throats were cleared in embarrassment.

Finally, Joe Willie heard the tape playing in his mind. He opened his mouth, and the words came out exactly as he had heard them. It was a brilliant speech, full of the right words, but he delivered it with no eye contact, no movements or gestures, no emotion. He felt dizzy and confused, but he got through it.

At the end of the speech, after a moment's pause, the crowd erupted with more cheers, more balloons, and more loud music. Joe Willie was the newly elected senator for the state of Arizona. Lillian took his arm and helped him toward a side exit before he blacked out.

#

Ronald, Samuel Gould, John Woods, Richard Rollins, Jack Ingersol, and Carl met in one of the suites at the Camelback Inn. The living room looked out over the green golf course and the distant mountains. Ronald was not enjoying the view.

"Jesus, Carl, he looked like a retard. I thought he was going to draw a damn blank. What the hell is wrong with him?" Furious, he poured another glass of Chivas.

Carl sat on the couch next to John Woods. "He's had too much, too many shots, too much travel. He's taking one or two shots every day. The last week of the campaign has been too much. He's been overdosed with mind serums."

"Well, you'd better come up with something. Plant the damn microchip if you need to. He has another Senate campaign and then a presidential campaign. He can't be looking like he did tonight. Shit." Ronald came and sat in the chair facing Carl. He was so angry he was panting.

Samuel Gould dared a comment. "Look, Ronald, he doesn't have to do anything for six years. He shows up to vote. He votes like we tell him to, maybe he serves on a rubber stamp committee. He'll mostly rest for six years. I'll use my publications and television to create the image that he's doing something wonderful."

Ronald began to relax. What Sam said was true; Joe Willie could stay out of sight and let Sam's public relations spin make him look like he was really doing something important.

Carl ventured an idea. "I could go to Nefaz and spend a month or so with Avery. We could improve on the mood shots and the microchip for his next campaign. If we get started on the formulas and the microchip now, Avery can have them perfected for his next run."

"Who'll keep him programmed while you're gone?" Ronald asked.

"I only need to be there a month, just long enough to get the formulas and the chip started. Then I'll be back with him. I can make up a supply of pills, enough for the month, and that'll keep him steady. We'll tell Lillian they're for fatigue. She can be sure he takes them."

Ronald looked at the Council members, who were nodding in agreement. "Okay, I'm going with you. I haven't been to the lab for a long time."

Ronald was a brilliant scientist and an expert in DNA modification. He got up and poured himself another drink. "Carl, you talk to Lillian. We'll fly back to the lodge tomorrow, and the ship can pick us up on Trail Ridge Road in the afternoon. We'll be on Nefaz by nightfall."

Samuel came to the bar and poured a vodka on the rocks. "I'll get going on a press campaign right away. He'll look like Superman when I'm through."

John Woods spoke up from his chair in the corner. "You know, we should be utilizing the lovely Miss Lillian. She could visit schools, Indian reservations, poor districts, spreading good will like crazy. She makes good press, and we can keep Dumbo in the background. Sam can make it look like it was all Joe Willie's idea."

"Good thinking." Samuel jumped to his feet, smiling. "Let me talk to her. I'll get going on his next campaign. It's never too soon. Lillian can carry the state for him if we use her wisely."

"Done. Gentlemen, our little robot is on his way to the White House." Ronald tossed off his drink. He could taste victory.

$ $ $

CHAPTER TWENTY-TWO

Joe Willie liked Washington, particularly Alexandria, where he could look at the handsome gay boys who ate in the restaurants and ran the shops. He was smart enough to know he was in a "look but don't touch" situation.

Lillian came once or twice a month, and they were visible at all the right events. She let him come to her bed a couple of times. He still didn't know how to please her, but he could bang away and get some relief for himself. With this outlet, he had stopped hitting her.

Carl came in with a little green bottle. "Time for your shot, Joe Willie," he sang out cheerfully.

"Carl, just for today, please, no more shots. I'm sick of them. I don't want a shot today."

"Now, Joe Willie, you know you have to have a thinking shot. You're on the Interstate Beautification

201

Committee, and they're meeting this morning. This shot will help you concentrate and remember what they say."

Joe Willie felt a boiling rage. "No! Goddamn it, Carl, I won't take a shot today. I want to sleep." He got up and moved away from Carl.

"All right, let me give you a sleeping pill. I'll call and tell them you have the flu."

"Fine." Joe Willie flopped on the maroon recliner and switched on cartoons.

#

Ronald slammed the phone. "Joe Willie is getting worse. I'm going to Nefaz to put a charge under Avery. We need the new serums and the microchip that Carl and I helped him develop. We have to get this idiot acting normal." He went to the bar and poured himself a Scotch. It burned but felt good on top of his fresh chipmunk breakfast.

Samuel sat with his hairy legs on the coffee table, drinking coffee and reading one of his papers. "I'm meeting with Willie's Women. The name has a nice ring, doesn't it? They'll help us get the women's vote again, and some good press."

"Fine, fine. I'm going now. John, drive me up Trail Ridge." Ronald was pulling on his skin as he spoke. They needed to get Joe Willie stabilized.

#

The green fog made Ronald's eyes water. He would be glad when they moved their laboratory to Earth. He should take time to visit his wife. He didn't want to, but it had been a long time and he didn't want to make her angry. Battered males were common on Nefaz because the females were bigger, stronger, and liked having things their way.

Avery came to meet him. He had aged; humans had such a short life span.

"Avery, we need the chip and the new serums. We've worn out Joe Willie's system, and he's built up an immunity to the formulas we're using. When can we have either new formulas or the microchip implant?"

Avery looked at the floor and cleared his throat before he responded. "We ran into a lot more work than we expected…"

Ronald interrupted, "How much, Avery? How much and how soon?"

"Another million, and I could put full staff on it. I could have it by the end of the week, but it wouldn't be fully tested."

"I don't give a damn. Get it ready. Bring it to the Earth lodge Saturday. Avery, it better stabilize him. He's getting harder to handle, and we still have another Senate campaign and a presidential campaign coming up. He has to appear human, at least coherent. He's like a damn zombie."

"Years ago we sent one of the boys from Joe Willie's litter to Utah. He's doing well, needs very few shots. He and Joe Willie were friendly here. Why don't you get them together? Maybe Joe Willie needs a friend."

Humans—they thought love and affection were the answer to everything. Ronald turned to leave, but then thought about how desperate they were to get Joe Willie straight. "Litter? Strange way of putting it. What's his name?"

"Representative Dwayne Rogers, lives in Salt Lake City. He comes off as a real human, needs very little in the way of mood altering shots to function. And they do come in litters—two to five per mother after we implant. We get similar characteristics in each baby. Rogers just turned out to be more human than Joe Willie. He's articulate, charming, and well-liked by humans in Utah."

"I'll get him and arrange for him to meet Joe Willie. Now get me the chip and the serum. No extra money until I have both." He spun on his heel and walked toward the ship, gazing out at the depressing fog and trying not to inhale the scent of the decaying planet. If they didn't succeed, Ronald's race would die out. He alone carried the burden of succeeding. He was finding it difficult to keep his confidence in Joe Willie as the next president.

Ronald decided not to visit his wife. The sight of her huge, hairy body no longer appealed to him. He had begun to prefer the smaller, frailer Earth women.

Humans had that part right. He hated the fact that the Nefaz females dwarfed the males. It was no wonder they couldn't wear skins and pass for human, as he and the Power Council did. No matter, he needed to get back to Earth. He'd see her soon enough.

#

Joe Willie had been taking the new serum for about a month when he flew back to Arizona for some R&R. He was feeling mellow. Carl dozed in the back seat of John's Lear. Joe Willie looked out at the landscape and began to feel better as the Grand Canyon came into view. He liked his desert home. He was anxious to take Devil Dog and ride up to Studder's grave. He hoped Lillian would be glad to see him.

The family limousine was waiting for him at the Sedona airport. "Have a good rest, Joe Willie," John said, shaking his hand as he left the plane.

"Aren't you coming to the ranch?"

"No time, we're making plans for your second campaign."

Joe Willie felt his eyes tear. "Do I have to? John, I hate it."

"This time will be better for you. The new shots are working, and Carl will implant a memory chip. Dwayne Rogers is coming out this weekend to meet you. Do you remember him from Nefaz?"

"Sort of, but that was such a long time ago." Joe Willie walked down the steps to the limousine. Carl followed, carrying his black bag of concoctions.

Lillian was on the steps with Janice and a black Labrador puppy. When Joe Willie saw the puppy, his heart sank. He knew it was a replacement for Devil Dog.

As Joe Willie got out of the car, the puppy came charging at him, nearly toppling over. Joe Willie knelt and let the puppy kiss and nip him with its sharp new teeth. Lillian and Janice came down the steps to greet him.

"Welcome home, son," Janice said, giving him a warm hug.

"Where's Devil Dog?" His voice cracked, and he brushed aside a tear.

"He's up with Studder. This is Pres. Lillian and I thought it was time for a new name. Is that okay?"

Joe Willie bent and picked up the wiggly black furball. He held him out and looked him in the eye. "Pres. I like it." As he hugged the puppy, tears flooded his eyes.

Lillian came and took Joe Willie's arm as he set Pres down. "If you want, I'll ride up to Studder's grave with you, so you can say good-bye to Devil Dog."

Joe Willie was surprised. "I'd like that. I'd really like that. Let me change, and we'll go."

Arm in arm, the three of them walked up the steps to the house. Pres nipped at their heels, his tail wagging enthusiastically.

#

Lillian found her Levi's and denim shirt at the back of her highest closet shelf, alongside her boots. She hadn't ridden since Tom's death. She hadn't been to the barn or to his cabin except for the day she had helped Tammy and her mother pack his belongings.

She watched Joe Willie as she descended the stairs. He seemed different today, more subdued, almost gentle. Maybe the new serum was working.

Janice was talking to him while Pres sniffed furiously at Joe Willie's old boots. "Don't you look wonderful?" Janice said to Lillian. "It's good to see you in your riding rags."

"It feels good to be in them again." She turned to Joe Willie and noticed he had a new white Stetson. He looked sort of cute, like a little boy. "Nice hat."

He tried his smile, which still came off as a sneer. "You like it? I may never take it off."

They walked toward the barn, Pres yapping and chasing after them on his awkward puppy legs. The Arizona sun was warm, and the smells from the barn rose to greet them. She looked at Tom's cabin and felt tears come to her eyes. Swallowing hard, she turned her eyes toward the barn.

"You want the pinto?" Joe Willie asked.

She nodded, not trusting herself to speak. She had ridden the pinto on the last day of Tom's life.

They rode alongside the creek bed and started up the canyon to the graves. Lillian didn't know where they were buried, but the path was the one she always rode with Tom, the path to their private place at the top of the red canyon.

"Pres, go back. Go on, you can't come." Joe Willie swivelled in his saddle, trying to make the young pup turn back. Not a chance.

"Let him come," Lillian said. "He wants to be with you."

"He's too little. He can't go that far."

Pres kept coming. They rode quietly, listening to the whisper of the cottonwood leaves and enjoying the song of canyon wrens. Lillian turned to look back and saw Pres flopped in the middle of the trail, exhausted.

"Joe Willie, look."

"Damn it, I told you he was too little." He turned his horse and went back to pick up the puppy. He partly unbuttoned his shirt and stuffed Pres inside. The dog rode the rest of the way comfortably snuggled against Joe Willie's belly.

Lillian laughed. "You are a softy, aren't you?"

"Yeah, for animals, I guess I am."

They rode in silence again, and her thoughts returned to Tom. She knew this ride was her farewell to him. She had to get on with her life.

"What's it like to be in love?"

Joe Willie's question rocked her. He had never talked about feelings or love. She looked at him with his new white Stetson, new puppy, and perhaps a new attitude. "It's like a roller coaster ride. You're caught up in it, out of control. One minute you're so high you can reach the stars, and the next you're spinning toward Earth. Love is full of twists and turns. It's a wild, exhilarating ride, and when it's over, you think about how short it was. You're left afraid, but you want to do it again."

"Wow, it must be great. I've never been in love. No offense, but... I guess I just don't know how to love."

Lillian felt her heart go out to this strange little man who was her husband. "Maybe someday you will. Joe Willie, you know our deal is for me to help you get elected president. I'll do whatever I can to help, because that was our arrangement. But if you ever find someone who takes you on a roller coaster, I'll step out of our marriage, and you can be with her."

He glanced over at her. "I don't think that's possible, but thanks."

They let the silence come in again, except for the clop of hoofs. They rode comfortably together to the top of the canyon rim. Lillian realized they were going to the place where she had consummated her love with Tom. She dreaded it, and yet looked forward to letting go of the past.

"Joe Willie, where were you born?"

He seemed surprised by her question. "I don't know. Ronald came and got me from a home. I guess it was an orphanage or a group home of some kind. Why?"

"I'm nosy. What state was it in?" Lillian's private detective had not been able to find any birth record. She found that strange.

"I don't know. No one ever told me. They just told me to forget where I came from, and I guess I did. I don't see how it matters."

She decided to drop the subject. Joe Willie was getting agitated, like he always did when he didn't know the answers and didn't understand. Still, she'd like to know. It was strange that no one knew where he had come from.

They arrived at the top of the canyon, and there, near the rock where she and Tom had committed to their love, were two mounds. Each had a small flagstone marker bearing the name of one of Joe Willie's best friends.

Joe Willie let Pres out of his shirt, and the dog sniffed around the graves and chased after a lizard. Lillian looked out at the vast valley filled with elaborate sandstone formations. She silently said good-bye to Tom, then rode a short distance away to give Joe Willie some privacy for his own good-byes.

\#

Joe Willie knelt down near the mounds and thought about the elegant white stallion and Devil Dog number three.

"You know what, guys, I wish I could join you," he said softly. "I hate what they're doing to me. The shots are making me crazy. I don't know how to be a senator. I don't know how to be anything. I wish I had a mound right here beside you." He brought his hands to his face and sobbed briefly. After a few minutes, he wiped his eyes. "I have to go now. They want me to run again for the Senate. I hope I get defeated. Of course, there's not a chance of that, not with all the money the Council will pour into my campaign. Wait for me. I'll be coming soon."

Joe Willie scooped up his panting puppy, waved Lillian to join him, and headed back to the house.

When they reached the barn, Joe Willie was surprised to see an old rusty Ford pickup and a horse trailer parked near the corral. Leaning on the truck, watching them approach, was Jeb.

"Who's that?" Lillian asked as she unsaddled.

Jeb was walking toward them. Already Joe Willie was getting aroused, and he didn't want Lillian to notice. "Lillian, go to the house. I'll handle this."

She started to say something, but he cut her off. "Please, just go inside."

She left, nodding to Jeb as they passed each other. Jeb walked straight to Joe Willie. They had seen each other a few times since their encounter in his trailer. They always got drunk before they had sex, and that

211

way they could say they didn't remember. But Joe Willie remembered every time.

"Hey, Joe Willie, how's the senator from the great state of Arizona?"

"Jeb, you can't be here. What do you want?"

Jeb leaned on the corral and watched Joe Willie unsaddle his horse. "I need a favor or two, Senator."

"What?" Joe Willie approached the corral, hoping Jeb wouldn't see his erection.

"I got pretty banged up by a bull last year. I have to quit the rodeo, and I wondered if you'd take my roper. I won't need him anymore, but I want him to have a good home. You can afford him, and I can't." Jeb glanced over at the trailer, and Joe Willie saw his tears.

"Sure, let's unload him. He'll have a home here as long as he lives."

"Thanks."

They went to unload the horse. Joe Willie noticed how difficult it was for Jeb to walk. "What happened?"

"Damned bull spun out from under me, kicking and snorting, came down with both heels on my lower back and crushed four vertebrae. If that wasn't enough, he gored the shit out of my lung. I'm through, Joe Willie. I need to find a job—dish washer, janitor, something. I don't know nothing but rodeo." Jeb was crying.

"Get your horse out. I'll be right back." He ran to the house and found Janice sitting in the kitchen eating a salad. "Mom, loan me a thousand dollars."

"What for?"

"Never mind, just give it to me."

Janice went to the vault and come back with two thousand. "Here. You don't owe me anything. You're going to help your friend, aren't you?"

Joe Willie didn't answer. He joined Jeb, and together they led the bay roping horse to the corral.

"Go over to Jerome, get a little apartment," Joe Willie said, handing Jeb the money. "One of the guys there will hire you. You'll be at home with them. People will understand you."

"I don't know how to thank you, Joe Willie. Will you come see me?"

"Call me when you're settled in, and I'll come over."

Joe Willie watched Jeb limp to his truck. He thought maybe he felt as close to love as he ever had for any human.

#

Carl watched too, and called Ronald. "I think we could have trouble. It's the young bull rider. I think Joe Willie gave him money."

"Where's he going now?"

"He'll go over to Jerome to find a place, and if something isn't done, Joe Willie will be going over there to visit."

"Thank you, Carl.   Something will be done." Ronald slammed down the receiver.

#

Joe Willie stopped in Cottonwood for a beer on his way to see Jeb. A couple of locals were nursing beers in the bar and discussing the latest news.

"Boy, that was some fire in Jerome, wasn't it?"

"Yeah, poor guy just moved in, and kaplooey! The old gas pipes gave out. Blew him to hell and back."

"I suppose all those old buildings are ready to explode, huh?"

Joe Willie heard the news and decided never to open up to another human. He spent the rest of the day getting drunk.

$ $ $

CHAPTER TWENTY-THREE

George was in his sixth month as a freshman senator, and Judy was in her sixth month of pregnancy. She had insisted on making juice and coffee for them that morning, even though he could see that she was in a great deal of pain. He wished she hadn't gotten pregnant. Not that he wasn't thrilled at the thought of becoming a father, but it pained him to know that she was having so much difficulty.

Throughout the ordeal, Dr. Flynn had been like a granny goose hovering over his flock. He was found of Judy and was taking particularly good care of her. George had flown in from Washington and would join her at her appointment today because Dr. Flynn had insisted that he wanted to talk to both of them.

"Sit down, Judy," he said for the third time, finally taking her elbow and leading her to the sofa. "Let me get breakfast today."

She relented with a smile. "Okay, okay. I guess I will sit a minute. No coffee for me, just some juice."

George was concerned. Judy looked pale and limp. "What time is our appointment?" He had to fly back that night; tomorrow was the vote on his national sales tax bill, and it was going to be close. He wanted to be there to pitch his bill and cast his vote, but his heart was here with Judy.

"One o'clock. Don't worry, you'll make your flight."

He set their coffee mugs on the pine coffee table and took her hand. "It's not that, Judy. I'm a little anxious about your health. Now I wish we'd just adopted. If anything happened to you—"

"Shhh." She put a finger to his lips to quiet him. "Don't be silly. I'm fine. Dr. Flynn is the best obstetrician in the country." She pulled his hand to her round tummy and smiled at him. "Feel it?"

George was overcome with emotion as he felt a small movement under his hand. "Whoa! I think he's going to be a goalie. He just kicked a puck out of the net." George was overwhelmed with love for Judy and his unborn child.

Dr. Flynn asked George to wait in his office while he examined Judy. George thumbed through every magazine in the office, paced around the mahogany desk, looked at degrees on the wall, and glanced at his watch every few minutes. When an hour had passed, he called and changed his flight. He would leave the next morning at 7:00.

A few minutes later, Judy and Dr. Flynn came into the office. George hugged Judy and stared into Dr. Flynn's eyes, trying to read his mind.

"Please sit down, both of you." The doctor took off his glasses and rubbed his eyes as he sat behind his desk. He was over sixty, slim, and silver-haired. He sighed. "George, Judy is having a really tough pregnancy. She may not be able to carry the baby to full term."

George reached out for Judy's hand, and they both gripped each other as if their lives depended on this physical contact.

"What do you mean?" George croaked. "Should we abort? Can we?"

"Easy, George, I didn't say she couldn't. I said she might not be able to. Judy, you're going to have to stay in bed for the next two and a half months. Bed rest will give you a fighting chance to come to term and deliver two healthy babies."

"Two?" George looked at Judy, then at the doctor. "What two?"

Judy smiled. "We're having twins, George. We're going to have healthy twins. I'll stay in bed if that's what it takes."

"I'll take a leave from my office. I need to be here with you."

Dr. Flynn stepped around his desk and stood in front of George. "No, you're the last thing she needs. You'll drive her crazy. Martha and Hilda will take turns caring for her, and we have a full-time nurse moving into your house tomorrow. Believe me, George, she'll be better off with you in Washington than here. We men aren't worth shit when it comes to this kind of thing." He grinned, showing his perfect white teeth.

Judy laughed. "He's right. You'd make me nuts. You go back to the Senate and do your job. Let the womenfolk handle this."

"You're taking this well," George said, flustered. "Are you sure?" He looked from one to the other.

In unison, they replied, "We're sure!"

#

George went back to Washington and actively fought for his bill and other bills he felt would help the country. Much of what Bush had done had only helped the rich, while millions of lower- and middle-income citizens suffered for years as a result of the bills he and his oil cronies had rammed through. This was the first time there were enough Democrats in the Senate to vote in bills that would help forgotten Americans regain a life.

He was in touch daily and sometimes twice daily with Judy and Martha. Judy was following the doctor's orders to the letter. That was why George was so surprised when, two months later, he received an emergency summons during a roll-call vote. *Urgent*, the message said. *Call home at once.*

He ran out of chambers and punched the speed dial for his home in Colorado. Martha answered on the first ring. "George? Oh, George, come home right away. Judy is hemorrhaging. They just took her to the hospital, and I'm on my way there now. Vice President Kennedy called and said he would bring you in Air Force Two. He's waiting for you at the airport. George, hurry."

He was dumbstruck. His aide came out of chambers. "What's wrong, Senator?"

"Get me to Air Force Two, now!" he snapped.

His aide caught a security guard as they rushed from the building. "See that banged-up tan Honda? It's mine. Get an escort for it. I have to get the Senator to Air Force Two immediately. It's a family emergency."

#

Accompanied by a police escort, Governor Blair met the plane on the runway in Colorado Springs. A short time later, sirens blared and lights flashed as they neared the hospital. George leapt from the car and ran up the stairs, three at a time, to the maternity ward. He was out of breath and frantic when he saw Martha and Hilda in the waiting room.

"Where is she? Is she all right?"

Martha took him into her arms. "Calm down. She's with the doctor. He said to let him know when you got here. He wants to talk to you." She signaled the nurse's station. They had been waiting for him, and one of them rushed off to the operating room.

Dr. Flynn was there in a matter of minutes, dressed in scrubs and looking solemn. He had George sit on one of the vinyl chairs, and pulled one up for himself. "George, Judy has lost a lot of blood. I'm working to save all three of them, but I can't guarantee I'll be able to do so. You have to make a decision. Do I save Judy, or do I save the twins?"

"Jesus, save Judy!" George looked at the doctor as if he was insane to even ask.

Dr. Flynn stood up. "Very well. I'll get back as soon as I can. Pray, George."

George collapsed on the chair and sobbed. No man should be asked to make the decision he'd just made. Still, he could not envision a life without Judy.

Martha put her arms around him. Governor Blair stood staring at his son, too shocked to speak. Hilda sat on the other side of George and sobbed with him.

Five hours later, they had heard nothing. George and his father paced the small room, avoiding collision with each other through some unknown male radar. George looked at his watch. "Dad, why haven't we heard? This is horrible, not knowing."

"You're right. There is no excuse for this. I'm going to see the administrator." He left the room, and ten minutes later, a nurse in scrubs came out to talk to them.

"Dr. Flynn is nearly finished. He'll be out in fifteen minutes. He can give you the news. We're sorry to keep you waiting so long, but we're in a fight against time. Dr. Flynn is doing everything possible to save all of them. Please be patient a bit longer."

Her voice was firm, but George noticed she looked concerned and tired.

One hour later, Dr. Flynn came out. He looked exhausted, but he was smiling. He came straight to George. "Senator Blair, you have a new son and a new daughter. They're small, but they're healthy."

"Judy?"

"She is extremely weak. She lost a lot of blood. We're giving her transfusions. The next eight hours are critical. After that, we'll know if she'll make it or not. She's a fighter. I'm hoping for the best."

"I want to be with her."

"Of course." Turning to Martha and the governor, he said, "Governor, Mrs. Blair, go home. Get some rest. There's nothing you can do for her right now. She's not conscious, but George can sit with her."

Everyone hugged George. Even his father gave him a powerful embrace.

All night, George held Judy's hand as nurses came and went, putting up new bags of blood and insulin. All night Judy fought for her life. George held her hand and prayed. About four o'clock in the morning, his head bobbed and he started to doze.

"Been a rough night, hasn't it, kiddo? She's coming back to you. I thought she might run away with me, but she said no."

"Damn you, Matt. This isn't funny."

"No, it's not. She's coming around now. Hey, Father, what are you naming that nephew of mine?"

Judy opened her eyes. "George, are the twins okay?"

Tears welled up in George's eyes. "Oh Judy, I'm so glad you're alive. God, thank you. Judy, I love you." He leaned over her bed and kissed her cheeks, lips, eyelids, forehead.

"And the babies?"

"Dr. Flynn says they're little, but healthy and doing fine."

She closed her eyes. "Go see them. Go home and sleep. I need to rest."

"I'll go see them, but then I'm back here with you."

"Fine. Is it all right if we name them Matt and Martha?"

"You bet. Matt and Martha it is."

He kissed her gently and went to meet his new daughter and son.

The nurse rolled two little babies to the window so he could see them. Their small tags read "Blair, baby boy" and "Blair, baby girl." They were tiny but perfect. He counted their toes and fingers just to be sure.

George tapped on the window. "Hey, they have names. He's Matt, and she's Martha."

"We'll put those names on right away, Senator Blair." The matronly nurse gave George a magnificent smile.

He stared at his babies in complete awe. Martha opened her blue eyes. Both babies had sandy brown hair, a mixture of George's and Judy's. He remembered his promise. "I want you to always know that I love you both and I'm proud of you."

When he had once again joined Judy, he took her hand, leaned back in his chair, and fell asleep.

$ $ $

CHAPTER TWENTY-FOUR

Ronald poured a generous Chivas. He looked around the room where he had come so many times to cover up something Joe Willie had done. Governor Benton and three of the party leaders were meeting with the Council. Ronald addressed their primary concern.

"Every time we throw this Blair guy a pile of manure, he walks away with the pony. His image just keeps getting better and better."

Richard Rollins stood up and paced the room. "Now he has those two darling twins that give him nothing but favorable press. Last term in the Senate, he was aggressive, he got things done. He even won respect from some of our people. The Republican senators voted with him and gave him public praise. He's smart, handsome, and a statesman. Shit, now he has this made-in-America family. He's going to be one tough SOB to beat."

"Yeah, he's damn dangerous to our campaign." Samuel Gould took a long sip of his beer. "But, gentlemen, our man is meeting with Dwayne Rogers, and I have a feeling Dwayne will be real good for him. Dwayne is gregarious, smart, well-thought-of, and we're going to get him a Senate seat. He can be a big brother of sorts for Joe Willie. My papers will make sure Joe Willie gets good press."

Governor Benton went to his desk and looked at the calendar. "He's done well on Carl's new medication. He seems calmer, and since the incident with the cowboy in Jerome, he hasn't even gotten drunk. He's looking forward to meeting Dwayne. I think he's finally growing up."

Ingersol had the long-term plan rolled out on the conference table. "Look, we're on schedule. We'll buy him another term, with Dwayne and his new medicine helping him out. He'll be okay. Then there's the crusade of Willie's Women. They're gaining members and will be a major factor in the presidential campaign. Lillian is still bringing in good press. I think we're on target."

Ronald looked around the group. He and the Council members could not speak as freely as they did among themselves, because the Federalist leaders didn't know everything they had done to bring Joe Willie to this point in his run for the presidency. He spoke carefully. "So the consensus, as I hear you, is we do nothing to Blair right now, but continue to look for some dirt on him. We concentrate on Joe Willie's positives and successes this term, and save any smear crusade for the presidential campaign. Is that about right?"

Murmured agreement came from those assembled.

"Then the meeting is adjourned. We'll see how Joe Willie takes to Rogers. If that goes well, we'll be off and running for the next six years." Signaling that the meeting was over, Ronald went to the bar and freshened his drink. He gulped it down and followed after the departing Federalist leaders. "Benton, call as soon as you have a take on how Joe Willie and Dwayne hit it off."

"Will do."

#

Joe Willie sat in his Dodge truck at the Sedona airport, waiting for Dwayne Rogers to fly in from Utah. The Arizona sun was hot, the blue sky obscured in the west by magnificent thunder clouds. It would probably rain today.

Joe Willie saw the Lear coming in and realized Dwayne was piloting the plane. Damn, that was cool. Joe Willie wished he knew how to fly.

Though his memory was fuzzy, Joe Willie recalled Dwayne as a smart boy who had made him laugh. Dwayne had been full of devilish pranks.

Dwayne climbed down the steps and waved at Joe Willie. He was tall, nearly six feet, with brown hair, impish blue eyes, and a crooked smile. Joe Willie wished he could smile.

"Hey, Joe Willie! Long time, no see."

They shook hands, and Joe Willie immediately felt good about Dwayne. "Hey Dwayne, I didn't know you were so close. Utah? Jeez, we should have gotten together sooner. I'm glad you're here."

"That your truck?"

"Yeah. Neat, isn't it?" Joe Willie felt proud.

Dwayne threw his bag in the back and climbed in the passenger side. "What's for entertainment?"

Joe Willie felt important. He had never really had a friend or a guest. He hadn't thought to plan anything. "Uh, well, I thought we'd go for a ride at the ranch."

"Shit, later for that stuff. Where's the action in this town? You got women here? What's a guy have to do in Sedona, Arizona, Senator?"

Joe Willie was really warming up to Dwayne, though not like with Jeb and the other men he'd known. This felt more like—friendship. "There are some places with fine waitresses at Tlaquepaque."

"Don't ask me to pronounce it, but I'm willing to check it out."

They drove off together, and Joe Willie thought he felt better than he ever had before.

#

They had lunch in Sedona, then drove to Jerome and meandered through the town. Finally, they went to a cowboy bar in Cottonwood, where they found two willing women, a motel, and a night of wanton sex. Joe Willie was surprised he didn't want sex with Dwayne. He tried to match Dwayne's considerable expertise with the two girls. When Joe Willie and Dwayne finally left the motel room, Dwayne put $500 on the night stand. Both girls were passed out and exhausted.

"Whoa, Joe Willie, you're a real ladies' man. You put me to shame." Dwayne had his feet propped on the dashboard. "Take me to a shower."

Joe Willie drove to the ranch. He showed Dwayne to the guest room, and after their showers they met in the kitchen for coffee. Lillian and Janice were already in the breakfast nook.

"Hey, everyone, this is Dwayne Rogers, representative from Utah, and my new friend." Joe Willie felt like he was ten years old, bringing home a classmate.

"My God, Joe Willie, you told me your wife was beautiful, but I had no idea. Miss Lillian, I'm your humble worshiper," Dwayne said, bowing theatrically and kissing her hand. "From now on, your wish is my command. If he don't treat you right, miss, he answers to me."

Lillian giggled. Dwayne turned to Janice. "No, you just cannot be old enough to be a mother to this rogue of a senator. You must be his sister. My, the man does surround himself with the finest women." He smooched Janice on the cheek. "Where have you been all my life?"

Janice laughed aloud. Joe Willie had never felt such camaraderie. It was fun.

"Come on, cowboy, take me for a ride up that canyon so I can see your funny-shaped rocks. I bet they're no better than Bryce Canyon's." Dwayne was full of energy and wit. He turned to Lillian. "You coming, pretty lady?"

"No, Janice and I are going to Phoenix for some serious shopping."

"Our loss, right, Joe Willie?"

Joe Willie smirked as he donned his white Stetson.

#

Once out on the trail, Dwayne settled down a little and seemed to enjoy the ride.

"Dwayne, how do you do that?"

"Do what?"

"I don't know, you just seem to know what to say. You're relaxed around people. You seem to be, uh, real."

"I heard that ever since you've been here, they've been giving you mood shots—one for this and one for that, right?"

"Yeah, but about six months ago I told them no more. Now they just give me one shot, and Carl planted a microchip in my brain. I'm sort of stabilized. I don't feel quite so spaced out, but I still don't fit in like you do."

Dwayne looped one leg over the saddle horn so he could turn toward Joe Willie. "When I got to Earth, I pleaded with my new parents not to give me shots. They didn't, bless 'em. They struggled through my hyperactivity and adjustment. I just take a calmer once in a while. Yours fucked you over with all those shots. Your poor brain is probably short-circuited. I heard from some of the other guys what they did to you."

Joe Willie was surprised. "You guys all kept in touch? How come I didn't know?" He was hurt.

"Ronald wouldn't allow it. You're the one for the presidency, and I guess they wanted to keep you separate. Ronald is the man. Whatever he says goes."

"Why do I need to be president?"

Dwayne stopped his horse and dismounted, dropping one rein so the horse could graze. Joe Willie followed suit, and they sat on a rock at the edge of the sometime creek.

"Joe Willie, Nefaz is dying. It was once a planet similar to Earth. They overpopulated it, creating that god-awful green smog with all their polluting. The Nefazian population is all but extinct. Ronald and the Council came here to take over Earth so they can bring what's left of their race here. They're creating a new Generian race, people like you and me. In order to take over Earth, they need to control the most powerful country, the U.S. of A. That's where you come in.

They needed a puppet for president, someone they could absolutely control, so when they brought you here they experimented with the serums, kept you away from the rest of us. Now they've scrambled your brain, and they're afraid you won't be able to win the presidency. So they decided to bring me in to help you. Man, I hope you do win, because they really screwed you over."

Joe Willie jumped up and kicked a rock into the dry creek bed. "Why should I even try? Why should I help them, after what they did to me?"

"Because, Joe Willie, you and me, we're Generians, created by the Nefaz. We need to commit to the party, or they'll simply eliminate us. It's not so bad. Don't fight them."

"But I don't know how to be the president. Hell, I don't know how to be a senator. They tell me how to vote, and I go and vote. That's all I do."

"That's going to change. I'm going to win a Senate seat for Utah, and I'll be in Washington with you. If you'll let me, I'll help you fit in, show you the ropes, create some good press for you."

"Man, that would be fantastic. What's in it for you?"

Dwayne grinned his funny lopsided grin. "Why, Mr. President, I'm going to be your vice president."

"Wow. Can you teach me to grin like you do? All I get is a smirk."

"Joe Willie, I can teach you all sorts of stuff. Stick with me, man."

231

They high-fived each other and mounted their horses. Joe Willie thought that even his horse stepped higher because Dwayne was there.

Joe Willie mulled over everything Dwayne had told him. He decided he would try really hard this term to be a good Federalist senator. He wanted to asked Dwayne about his feelings for men, but decided this was not the time.

$ $ $

CHAPTER TWENTY-FIVE

Judy learned that three-year-old twins could be both a blessing and a curse as she answered yet another of their unending questions.

"Why do bees have to sting?" Martha quizzed.

"Because they're girls," Matt chimed in.

"Are not! … Are they, Mom?"

One good thing about twins was that you didn't have to answer every question, because they often answered each other. Taking their hands, Judy led them on a walk to Grandmother Martha's house.

"Bees are both boys and girls," Judy explained. "They sting to protect what's theirs."

"Really? Why don't they have to share?" Matt was often reminded to share when he took all the newest toys.

"Because they're bees, dummy," Martha chided.

Shaking her head and smiling, Judy delivered the twins to Hilda and went to join Grandma Martha for coffee and some adult conversation.

Martha and Hilda had been terrific. Never allowing Judy to hire help for the twins, they had taken them while Judy worked to build her probate/estate planning practice at the Burney, Lundquist & Blair firm on South Tejon.

"Martha, talk to me in Adult, please."

Martha smiled as she poured her daughter a cup of coffee. "I'd rather talk in Mother. I'm so proud." She turned the morning paper so Judy could read the article.

Halfway into his first term as Colorado senator, George Blair has been praised by both parties and Vice President Kennedy for the passage of his Adopt-a-Senior program. After the Bush Social Security investment plan failed, many seniors across the country were trying to survive on five hundred dollars a month. Senator Blair created a plan whereby sports figures who were making obscene amounts of money were encouraged to adopt a senior and guarantee them one thousand dollars a month for ten years. The seniors can now afford food and prescriptions. The sports figures, of course, receive a tax break and endorsements. Senator Blair can be credited with a win-win bill. There is no opposition from any of the three major parties. Well done, Senator.

Judy was beaming. "Has Matthew seen this?"

"I assume he has." She had barely finished speaking when Judy took the paper and took off to the governor's home office.

"The door was open," she said. "I took that as an invitation to come in."

Matthew Blair, senior stood and came to take her hands. "My door is always open to you, Judy. What can I do for you?"

She showed him the paper. "Have you seen this?"

"Yes, I read it this morning. Fantastic work, isn't it? He's going to be an excellent president."

"Glad you feel that way. Now call him and tell him how proud of him you are."

"Now?"

"Now."

He reached for the phone, looking surprised when Judy remained in the room.

"George, how are you?" He cradled the phone, still looking at Judy. She stood her ground.

"I wanted you to know that was great work on the Social Security bill. Keep up the good work, Senator Blair." After exchanging a few more pleasantries, he hung up.

"You just can't say the words, can you?" Judy said, disgusted. "Someday you'll have to tell him you're proud of him and that you love him. He needs to hear it."

He grinned. "He knows, Judy. Men don't have to say all that stuff. Anyway, now that I've been a good father, can I go play with my grandson and granddaughter?"

"You haven't quite made it as a good father, but yes, you can play with the twins." Judy left shaking her head. She didn't understand why he couldn't tell George that he was proud of him.

#

George finished his first term and would run unopposed for his second term. There was no contender from the Democratic Party, and there was no one of major importance running for either the Republicans or the Federalists.

He was enjoying politics and looked forward to running again, but his family was the true love of his life. He seemed to have a perfect marriage. Tomorrow he was going home for two weeks of camping in the high country with Judy and the twins. On top of it all, he and his father had grown closer, though his father had yet to say he was proud of him.

His phone rang as he was finishing some last-minute notes. Judy's voice sounded panicky. "George, your father passed out today, and we rushed him to Penrose Hospital. The tumor's come back. Can you get here tonight?"

George sank down on his bed. Every time he thought he had the world by the tail, it turned around and bit him. "How bad is it?"

"I don't know yet. Call me on my cell as soon as you arrange a flight. George, I think you better get here quickly."

"How is Mom?"

"I have her right here in my arms. Martha, do you want to talk to George?" There was a moment's pause. "She said she's too upset. Just get here."

He hated to take advantage of friends, but he called Vice President Kennedy.

"I'll call my Lear pilot," Kennedy said. "It'll be faster and less conspicuous than Air Force Two, and don't apologize. You get home and take care of your father. Call if there's anything we can do."

Once more, George was in the air praying his father would live. At least they had been closer since the birth of the twins. He knew his father would never share with him what he had shared with Matt, but he felt less needy than before. The term as senator had convinced him that he was a capable man and needed validation from no one.

#

George was rushing down the hall toward the waiting room just as the doctor came out of surgery to speak to them. George gave Martha and Judy a quick kiss, and the three of them stood with arms around each other as they faced the doctor.

"The tumor is back," the doctor explained. "We thought we had it all, in fact we may have gotten all of it, but sometimes they grow back. It's much larger than it was before, and I don't think you should decide right away on surgery. It could leave him paralyzed, or worse… he might not make it through the surgery."

Martha collapsed on the sofa, sobbing. Judy went to her, and George walked the doctor away from them. "What do you suggest we do?"

"I think, Senator, that you should take him home tomorrow and let him rest a few days. He's lucid. You need to sit as a family and make some tough decisions. If we operate, his situation could get worse. We can try radiation treatments and see if that helps. I'm sorry. I can't paint a pretty picture. I think he may have to step down as governor."

"Thank you, Doctor. We'll leave him here tonight and take him home in the morning. Can I see him now?"

Martha insisted she would stay the night with her husband, and there was no point in arguing with her. George and Judy made a brief visit to his room, and Martha took a chair beside his bed.

George was exhausted. He kissed Martha and said, "We'll be back first thing in the morning, Mom. Are you sure you're okay?"

Martha nodded. "Go on now, see the kids and get some sleep. We'll see you in the morning."

During the night, Governor Blair slid into a coma. The next morning, George could barely stay on his feet when he heard the news from Martha.

"That can't be. How could this happen? The other doctor didn't say anything about a coma."

Judy put her arms around Martha. "Martha, let me take you home for a rest."

"No, I want to be here."

"Go with Judy," George said. "Take a shower, have some good coffee, and then come back. I want to be alone with him."

Martha started to resist, but Judy took her hand and gently led her away.

George went to his father's bedside. He looked so peaceful, even with the assortment of tubes and drips. He looked old. George took his hand. "Don't go yet, please. I want to tell you I love you. I want you to see me in the White House. I want to be your son awhile longer." George didn't fight the tears.

"He's not coming back. He'll hang around awhile, but he'll never be whole again."

"No, Matt, this time you're wrong."

"Kiddo, I wish that was so. He has a little time here. You can let him know about the love you have for him, but he won't be able to respond. You'll really have to love him for the next bit of time."

"How long?"

No answer came. Matt was gone.

#

They converted the governor's home office into a bedroom. Being confined to his wheelchair, he had to be on the main floor for ease of transport and caring. Besides, he seemed to like it there.

Two days after his father's collapse, George made the phone call to the governor's office in Denver and arranged to meet with state officials that afternoon.

George paced around the governor's office as the party leaders waited to hear his urgent message.

"Gentlemen, my father is in a coma."

The men gasped. "Jesus, when? How? What happened?"

George gave them the details. They immediately set in motion a confirmation of the next-in-line as governor, then began discussing whether to run George for the Senate or for governor. George was angry that these men, who had been his father's friends for years, immediately began scheming about George's career upon news of the governor's incapacitation. George made the decision for them.

"I'll tell you what I'm going to do—I'm returning to the Senate. That's what my father would want, and it's what I want. I'm your man, and I'll be your presidential candidate, but I belong in the Senate, and that's where I'm going."

None of them opposed his decision.

That weekend, he sat with his father in his former office, watching Colorado College play North Dakota.

George often glanced over at his silent father and wondered if he knew how much his son loved him.

Election day came and went, and George recaptured his seat by a landslide. Public adoration for the Blair family was high in the state of Colorado and many neighboring states as well.

$ $ $

CHAPTER TWENTY-SIX

Joe Willie won his second term easily with the help of his new serum, the implanted microchip, Lillian's good press, Dwayne's encouragement, the Council's spin and money, and the groundswell of Willie's Women.

The wind whistled, the sky threatened rain, and the orange and red autumn leaves trembled as they cascaded to the ground. Washington D.C. was entering fall. Joe Willie and Dwayne hailed a cab at the airport.

"So, where's your apartment?" asked freshman senator Dwayne Rogers.

"Carl and I stay in Alexandria."

"No, no, my boy, they'll think you're gay. You can't live there. You'll get a place where I am. The Watergate is much more respectable. Boy, I have to teach you everything." He grinned his lopsided grin and punched Joe Willie playfully on the shoulder.

Joe Willie nodded agreement. He had come to rely on Dwayne for everything. Dwayne had traveled with him on his second Senate campaign, helping him get through speeches and even coming up with the idea to make the white Stetson a trademark. It would suggest Joe Willie was a down-to-earth good ol' boy. Joe Willie himself had added his trademark salute of a cocked thumb and pointed finger, as if he was shooting a gun.

Dwayne had also managed to win a Senate seat from Utah, and now the two of them were going to make themselves known in the Senate.

"It'll be good to be involved this term. Last time I was so bummed out on shots, but this term, with you helping me, I'll be a good senator."

"Yeah, and I know all the spots where we can hide out and screw women and never get caught. Why you'd want to, with Lillian in your barn, beats me." Dwayne shook his head.

"Hey, I'm more man than one woman can handle." Joe Willie would die of embarrassment if Dwayne knew Lillian hadn't let him in her bed for several years. He had also decided he'd never let Dwayne know how much he had enjoyed being with Jeb and a few other men. He was straight now, he was sure, and committed to becoming the Federalist president.

#

George thought of Judy and the twins as he walked into his Watergate apartment. The twins were the ones who could bring life to his father's dull eyes. When he wasn't campaigning, George spent as much time as he could with his family. Judy continued to build her practice and handle both family estates, and she was damn good at it.

The phone rang and interrupted his brooding. "This is Senator Blair."

"Hi, Ray Kennedy here. I need a favor."

"Anything for you, Ray. Name it." He owed Vice President Kennedy personally and politically, and he really meant it when he said he would do anything for him.

"We want you to chair the committee on Social Security and tax reform. There's a good chance, with the make-up of the House and Senate this term, that we'll finally get through the initiative to increase entitlements so seniors won't have to rely on the Adopt-a-Senior program. That'll do away with the fiasco Bush created with his gimmees for the rich. If we can win this round, we can tackle income tax and finally eliminate the IRS completely. If that happens, we can hand you the presidency."

"Jesus, yes. You know I wanted that committee. How'd you swing it? Maybe I don't want to know."

Kennedy laughed. "You don't want to know, but we do want you over to our Georgetown apartment for dinner tonight. Eight o'clock?"

"See you then, and Ray, thanks again."

#

The night before the Social Security vote, Judy flew in to be with George. He had begged her to bring the twins, but she won out. "Martha wants to keep them with your Dad. They're the only joy in his life, you know. Besides, I want some adult time with you, Senator Blair. I don't think the children should hear you begging for more."

"Enough, already. I'm convinced." George was smiling at the thought of romantic time with Judy. "If you hurry, I can ravish you before dinner."

"Just you and me? A romantic dinner?"

"Not quite. It's an unofficial caucus to verify votes to carry the Social Security bill. I think we have it."

"George, that's wonderful. I'll be in at five, time for a little teaser before dinner. Love you."

"Love you too." George figured Judy was smiling as she hung up, like he was.

#

Ronald and Samuel Gould were naked in the deep woods, looking for a kill. They hadn't had much time to satisfy their natural urges. Most of their time was spent making enough money to keep their run at the presidency viable. Even though they controlled about

245

sixty percent of the world's wealth, getting a cretin elected president took a great deal of money.

"That damn Blair guy, he just keeps getting stronger and going up in the polls. Some of our people even like him. We should get rid of him." Samuel was keeping an eye on the bushes and tree branches as they made their way through the thick spruce grove.

"Too obvious. We're lucky Carl didn't get caught at the hospital when he gave the governor that shot. My God, he did it while the guy's wife was sitting right there, holding his hand. We're lucky no one made the connection to the coma. It's just too risky."

"You really think we can get more votes for Joe Willie?"

"Samuel, Samuel, how long have we been at this? With our money, your communication holdings, and our control in the key states, how can we lose? This election will go so smooth it'll make the rigged 2000 election look like a neighborhood stick ball game. We'll win, hands down."

"And none too soon. Nefaz is barely liveable. We need to get our lab relocated ASAP. Our women are raising hell because they want to get back down here. They do love those Northwest forests."

At that moment, they both spotted the deer. They crashed through the thick undergrowth, and in seconds they had downed the buck and were enjoying warm blood and fresh red meat.

#

Joe Willie's second term ended without fanfare. He had done a respectable job of serving with Dwayne on some minor committees, and he had showed up regularly for roll call and voting. He had come to depend on Dwayne for his women, his repartee, and his friendship. Carl had added smart shots to Joe Willie's treatment, and the microchip seemed to improve his memory, all of which helped him speak intelligently during dinners and meetings. The Council was in full gear preparing for the Federalist run to the White House. Yet despite his success, Joe Willie secretly wished he was back in Arizona, up on the mesa top with Studder and Devil Dog.

George Blair ended his second term in a blaze of glory. The Social Security bill had passed, and the IRS would soon be history. The professional players from all the major sports voted to continue the Adopt-a-Senior program. George met with party leaders to map out convention strategy, then went home to spend time with his father, Judy, and the twins. He wished his father could share his joy at being nominated as the party's candidate for the presidency.

#

Ronald had the Republican candidate's suite and the convention hall bugged with sound and video so they could monitor everything. He watched from the lodge as Joyce Unger examined herself, still wet from the shower, in the full-length bedroom mirror. At forty-five, she still looked good for a human. Water gleamed on her firm, dark skin and dripped onto the green bath mat. She didn't deserve the treatment the Republican Party was giving her, but she would go down in history as the first black woman ever to achieve such an honor. Ronald almost admired her.

"You ready?" said Cornell, her husband of twenty years. He came in and began drying her back. Ronald was aroused as he watched the sensual moves between them.

"Ready for some things, perhaps, not ready for my acceptance speech." She looked over her shoulder, and her brown eyes raked over his handsome body. "In that tux, my God, I'll need another shower."

Cornell laughed as he continued drying her back and nuzzling her neck. "You've come a long way, Congresswoman. I want you to know I'm proud of you."

She turned and looked steadily into his eyes. "I'm a lucky woman to have you. But this nomination is nothing to be proud of. I'm being used, and I know it. The party is so damn desperate."

He put a finger to her lips. "No, I won't hear you talk like that. Get dressed. We'll have time for a quick toast downstairs before we go to the floor."

Ronald watched as she came into Cornell's arms. "Damn, Cornell, the Republicans were asked not to have their convention in three states. Texas was still reeling from the Bushes, Florida was still tainted by the crooked 2000 election, and California laughed at them. They had to settle on South Carolina."

"Yeah, we are a sorry party, but we have the prettiest candidate."

She slid a silky blue silky gown over her head and let it cascade to the floor. She looked at herself in the mirror. Ronald had to agree that the gown gave her quiet elegance. Finishing her make-up and jewelry, she took Cornell by the hand and left for the convention hall.

Ronald switched the surveillance video to the convention hall so he could hear her speech.

"Ladies and gentlemen." The crowd roared as Joyce and Cornell appeared on the stage. The red, white, and blue balloons soared to the ceiling. The band played a Dixie tune, and the people rose to their feet with wild applause, stomping, and cheering.

"Ladies and gentlemen, I give you the next Republican president of the United States, the first woman president of our great nation, Joyce Unger." More screaming. Barbara, her campaign manager, stepped back as Joyce came to the podium.

Joyce looked out at the sea of faces. Ronald knew that even though her nomination had come out of the party's desperation, it must still be a thrill to be the first African-American woman ever nominated for the highest office in the land. He smirked. Too bad she would soon be out of it.

She stood smiling and holding her hands in the air for silence. The crowd, mostly paid delegates, roared and clapped.

"I thank you, every one of you, for the opportunity to lead our great party in the race the of century. I know many out there do not give us a prayer to win. Well, let me tell you, they are in for the fight of their lives. In the words of Martin Luther King, I have a dream."

The crowd erupted again. By the time she had concluded her twenty-minute acceptance speech, Ronald could tell by the enthusiasm that a few of the party loyalists had begun to think they might have an outside chance against Joe Willie and George Blair. He laughed, knowing this election was already bought and paid for.

Cornell came out of the wings and stood with Joyce, smiling and waving. Her son and daughter came on stage and joined them, hugging and waving. It was a proud moment for Congresswoman Unger.

#

George was in the closet scattering clothes on the floor, searching for the perfect shirt and pants. The pile of discards kept building as he tore clothes off and replaced them with new ones. He smiled, remembering many years ago when his mother had helped him dress for Judy.

"George, go to the bedroom and let me find you something to wear." Judy was resplendent in her royal blue chiffon gown. Age had been kind to her. She still looked like a young Miss Colorado.

"Thanks. I'm nervous. I'll review my speech while you find some clothes that make me look presidential."

A few minutes later, Ray Kennedy, who had half-heartedly challenged George for the nomination, called to tell George he was stepping out of the race. He had been a good vice president, but was not strong enough to carry the party's vote for nominee.

"I'll throw my support behind you and give you my endorsement tonight. You're the man, George. Take us to the White House."

George had stammered, "Thanks." Then he tossed out an idea. "Ray, I want you to think about this before you answer. I haven't discussed this with anyone, but I wonder if you would consider being my running mate."

"Uh, well, I'll have to get back to you on that. I'm flattered, but the party will have some say. Damn, George, I'm speechless." He laughed. "Might just work. We'll talk later. Congratulations."

George was still pondering why he had been so impulsive, but Ray Kennedy made good sense. He had Washington experience, he had White House experience, he was a strong party leader, and who said he couldn't be vice president to two different presidents?"

Little Matt and Martha ran into the room, acting like ten-year-old kids but looking like little adults in their matching blue linen outfits. Martha's was a calf-length dress with tiny spaghetti straps, and Matt's was a suit set off by a rose-colored shirt and navy tie. "Hey, Pop, how do we look?"

Matt had picked up the nickname Pop from somewhere and loved to tease George by saying it whenever he could. George feigned disapproval, but loved it.

"You're so rude. He's your father, not your 'pop,' dummy." Martha came to twirl in front of George for his approval. "Do I look as pretty as Mommy?"

"Absolutely. You both look wonderful. I'm so proud of you, and I love you." This statement had become his mantra. He had wanted so much to hear those words from his own father.

Judy came with his new silk navy suit, smiling as she observed the scene. "Mr. President, your ensemble." She turned to Matt and Martha. "Come here, let me see." She looked them up and down. "What do you think, Pops? Will the children pass inspection?" Both kids giggled.

George felt his eyes tear. My God, he was going to be named Democratic nominee for president of the United States, and he had a family he loved and who adored him. The only thing missing was his father's presence in all of it. Martha had flown to Denver to be with them. She rarely left Matthew alone, but George wanted her to see him accept the nomination. Hilda had stayed behind to take care of the former governor.

He shooed all of them from the room and began dressing. He wanted to center himself before he went to the convention floor. Judy stayed behind and closed the door. She put her arms around his waist. "I love you so much. We're on our way to the White House. I'm so proud of you, and so is your father."

"I don't need his approval anymore, Judy. It would be nice, though, if he could share this moment with us." He broke free to pull on his shirt. "I asked Ray Kennedy to veep for me."

"That's ingenious. Has the party okayed it?"

"No, it just came to me. But I think he'd be good."

"Beyond good, it's perfect. You two will be unbeatable."

"The Federalists have more money."

"Yeah, but their candidate is an asshole." Judy did not often use such language, and George was amused by her venom.

In a mock drawl, he answered, "Why, honey, he's just a Friendly Federalist, come to unite the world."

Martha peeked in. "Can I have a quick hug from the future president?"

As he pulled her to him, the phone rang, and he motioned one of his aides to pick it up as he and Judy walked to the convention floor to give his acceptance speech. Martha waved aside the aide and picked up the phone.

"Hello?"

"Martha? Oh, Martha." Hilda was sobbing hysterically.

Martha felt her heart drop toward her stomach. She knew the answer to her question before she asked. "What is it, Hilda?"

"He's gone, Martha, he just went to sleep, and—" Hilda's voice broke. "And never woke up. I didn't have time to call anyone."

Somehow Martha kept her composure for the next few moments. "Hilda, it's all right. Calm down. I'll fly home as soon as George gives his speech. I don't want to ruin this moment for him."

After hanging up, she dabbed her eyes, took a deep breath, and went to join her son and his family.

#

George's speech had the hall rocking. Cheers, balloons, "Hail to the chief!" and all. The Democrats were pumped and confident they had the man to win in the fall. He stood with his arm around Judy on one side and Martha on the other. The twins were in front, waving and smiling. Flashbulbs popped, cameras rolled, and the Blair legacy was in full swing.

"Way to go, kiddo."

George shook his head. He didn't want to talk to a ghost while receiving his party's adulation. He answered the voice silently. *Matt, you pick the dandiest times to show up.*

"Sorry, but there's someone here who wants to say something to you."

He heard the strong voice of his father, clear as if he was standing next to him. "Go get 'em, George."

The presidential candidate grinned wider and waved, but once more he felt the knife of life slice away a part of him, the part that had been his father. He knew his father was dead.

#

Phoenix won the bid to host the Federalist convention, and it had turned up the heat to 115 degrees in honor of the event. Lillian, Dwayne, and Joe Willie sat in their suite at the Camelback Inn waiting for the call from Joe Willie's opponent. Lillian looked at the two men and wondered why she was still with them. She had made a promise to her father, and she had honored it, but now she was tired of the game. She was glad Dwayne had come into her life. She didn't love him, but he filled a need in her. He made her laugh, and they enjoyed a sort of brother-sister camaraderie.

The night before, feeling a little guilty about years of turning Joe Willie away, she decided to try once more and invited him to her bed. He started out gentle and loving, but then, as usual, he turned violent. She ended up feeling as if she had been raped. "I hate you, I hate you! Get the hell out of my room and leave me alone!"

She yelled so loud, she was sure the aides heard her. Now she sat looking at the man who could make her first lady. Smiling, she saw herself walking down the stairs to greet the heads of state. She felt a mixture of hatred and desire to come into that much power and prestige.

Joe Willie was studying his acceptance speech while Dwayne sprawled on the couch, grinning mischievously. She was sure he knew of her encounter with Joe Willie last night.

The Federalists would nominate Joe Willie tonight as their candidate for the president. There had been no real opposition, and, surprisingly, Joe Willie's favorable ratings were solid. Lillian marveled at the Council's ability to keep the real Joe Willie hidden from the public.

"I'm going to dress," she announced to no one in particular.

Joe Willie was lost in the Teleprompter. Dwayne stood and walked toward Lillian. "I'll go get ready too, my lovely lady. Hey, President, you'd better get dressed."

"Not a good night last night?" Dwayne asked when they were alone in the elevator.

"None of your damn business." Suddenly she was irritated with both of them. They seemed to have been made from the same mold.

\#

As soon as the cheering subsided, Joe Willie stood silently at the podium, staring at the monitor before him. The crowd grew totally silent as the pause became embarrassingly long. Finally he began to speak, and miraculously he got through his ten-minute speech without a mistake. However, he also went through it with no emotion, like a robot. As always, the crowd still cheered. Willie's Women screamed, balloons erupted toward the ceiling, and the band played. Joe Willie was on his way to the White House. Lillian stood on stage in her red gown and waved adoringly to the delegates.

#

Ronald switched on the giant screen. He and the Council watched from the comfort of their lodge, where they could peel out of their skins and be themselves.

"Well, gentlemen, we finally have a man to take over the presidency. Within a year from his inauguration, we'll take over this planet." Ronald held up his Chivas. "Cheers."

Samuel cleared his throat as he poured himself another vodka. "I have a bit of bad news. The Republicans bought *What if America?* magazine, and I can't control what they print. I know they plan to run rumors and innuendoes, without any regard to the facts. It's a loose-cannon gossip column, and it'll be dirty. We'll have to watch them carefully."

257

Ingersol rubbed his round stomach. He had enjoyed a good hunt. "Not to worry," he said lazily. "We can use their lack of verifying sources to our advantage and slip some slander of our own into their new magazine. I also have it on good authority that before election day, Joyce Unger will bow out and endorse Joe Willie. Our bases are covered."

"That damn Blair, he gets good press from his father's death. Once again, he seems to be the all-American boy, the do-no-wrong superhero. Shit. Sam, can't you get some dirt on him?"

"Not much dirt to find. We'll have to start rumors and let them catch fire. We'll have to rely on spreading gossip, buying votes, and fixing some major states. Thank God they didn't do away with the electoral college after the 2000 fiasco. We can buy California's electoral vote. That'll give us the votes we need to win."

"If not, do we own enough Supreme Court judges to appoint him?" They all laughed at Richard's joke.

Ronald set his drink on the table. "There's no way we can be stopped. If anyone threatens our win, they'll be bought or eliminated."

Ronald saw his dream coming to fruition. He and the Generian race would take over Earth soon. "By the way, we have new skins. Let's get dressed. We'll have our final strategy meeting in Sedona." Ronald hated the new skins, but every five years they had to don a set that made them appear older. Ronald didn't like looking older.

Who Bought Joe Willie the Presidency?

$ $ $

CHAPTER TWENTY-SEVEN

George and Judy sold their smaller house and moved into the Blair mansion with Martha. They were remodeling Matthew's downstairs bedroom, turning it back into an office for George. The dark paneling gave way to new half-cut ponderosa pine walls; heavy maroon drapes were exchanged for aspen wood blinds. George had a skylight cut to bring in more light. Transformed, the office became his campaign war room.

"Hey, Pops, why don't we put the big screen in here?"

George loved the way Matt teased. He was so much like his uncle.

"Well, son, if I don't win the election, we might just do that."

"Matt, Martha, both of you out of here. Let your father work." George's mother came in for her first look at the newly remodeled room.

"Oh my, George, it's beautiful."

"Is it okay? You don't mind?" George had been concerned that she might be offended by the major changes he had made to her house.

"I told you, the house is yours to do with as you wish. I love what you've done." She opened the wood blinds, and sun poured in, warming the room. "You've become your own man. The old George would have left this place as a shrine to his father. I'm glad to see you stand on your own. You're out of the shadows of both Matthew Blairs."

George was surprised by her insight. He put his arm around her shoulder, and they stood together, gazing out over the city and the Broadmoor Hotel. "Yes, I'm my own man. They both contributed to who I am, and now I want to become the president—not for them, but because I think I can really make a positive impact on our country."

"You will, George. You will." She gave him a peck on the cheek and turned to leave. "I'll let you get to work. How many of the campaign leaders will we be having for dinner? I need to tell Hilda."

"Just the top five today. We're going to set the tone for the campaign."

He picked up the first issue of *What if America?* and turned to Kip Kipfer's first "Could it be?" article:

261

Well, America, for my first question, I have a real thought-provoker. We all know politicians are self-obsessed, self-serving, and without conscience. However, what would you think of a young man who was so greedy he would plot his own brother's death to make sure he would be in line to inherit the Blair political future?

No one could ever prove it, but rumor has it that George Blair might have let his own brother drown in order to move up the political ladder. It is a fact that all those many years ago, the Democratic Party was grooming Matt Blair for this year's presidential run.

Think about young George—jealous, ambitious, and hungry for attention. Could it be, America, that he let his own brother drown?

George threw the paper across the room. "Goddamn son of a bitch! I can't believe this!"

Judy ran into the room, alarmed. "What is it? Are you all right?"

Trembling, George stared at the magazine he'd thrown to the floor. He felt as if he might throw up. "Judy, look at this piece of shit. I can't believe the dirt is starting so soon, and that it's so vile."

Judy read the article. "We'll sue." She came to him and put her arms around his waist. "George, I'll fight the legal battle. You tend to the campaign. Your campaign team is here." Her voice was husky as she tried to control her anger. "I'll put this rag out of business."

She rolled up the magazine and left George pacing the war room.

#

Judy could not remember when she had been so angry. She went to her room and called Alvin, the senior partner at her firm. "Alvin, I want to file a suit against *What if America?* magazine. Have my secretary start on it. I'm coming in."

Alvin greeted Judy with a glass of brandy. "Judy, there's no basis for a suit. The magazine has disclaimers galore, and it doesn't pretend to tell the truth. It's a rumor mill by design. You'll never win a suit, and you'll just keep it grinding, which will keep George's name in the public mind in a very damaging way. Let it die."

Judy loved her boss, and his advice was probably correct. But she couldn't let them get by with this despicable attack on her husband.

"No, Alvin. Damn it, there must be something we can do."

Alvin laughed a low, rumbling laugh which she had come to adore. "There is. Let's invent some stories of our own about Joe Willie."

"George won't go there. He wants to run a clean campaign, above the dirt. He won't allow it."

"Then Mrs. Blair, I suggest we have a strategy meeting. We are not asking his approval. We'll run our own campaign in his best interests."

"He'll kill me if he finds out."

"George is a leader and a statesman, but he's not a politician. Do you want to be first lady?"

"Yes."

"Then let's get to it. You'll have to be the down-and-dirty politician in the family."

Judy sipped her brandy and made a commitment to George's campaign. She would do whatever it took to see that he became president.

The phone buzzed. Alvin punched the intercom and said testily, "I told you, no disturbances." He picked up the receiver and listened for a moment before hanging up. "Judy, there's a woman here from Arizona who says she has information to sell that would harm the Federalist candidate. I told my secretary to send her in. This may be just what we need."

Judy hoped so. She was still seething about the article that had so unfairly burned George.

Marilyn Smith had not grown into a pretty woman. She was twenty pounds overweight and wore tight jeans and a yellow plaid shirt several sizes too large. Her hair had been visited by many bottles of peroxide. As Alvin came from behind his desk to greet her, Judy took his seat behind the desk.

Alvin led Marilyn to one of the chairs in front of the desk and took the one beside her. He introduced her to Judy, and Judy made no attempt to shake hands.

"Now tell Mrs. Blair and me what you know about Joe Willie Benton."

"I'll want some money." Marilyn batted her eyes at Alvin, ignoring Judy.

"Tell us what you know, Marilyn. We'll discuss money after we hear what you have to tell us."

Alvin and Judy were not disappointed with what Marilyn had to share.

#

One month later, the campaigns were in full swing as all three candidates criss-crossed the country, appearing on the early and late talk shows and speaking wherever they could.

Ronald and the Council monitored all three campaigns and the daily polls. Joyce Unger was making a surprising impact. She would not win, but she was making headway with both of her opponents' Black and female voters.

Joe Willie, Lillian, and Dwayne were in Florida trying to sway the senior vote. Joe Willie was urging a return to the Bush plan of individual investment of Social Security money in stocks. It had been a disaster then, and many seniors had wised up, wanting nothing to do with it. After the ill-advised investment plan, most seniors realized all it meant was that they would take home a lot less in their Social Security checks. Many others were buying into the idea because they were living nicely on the additional income Blair's Adopt-a-Senior program had provided them. No one was talking about the fact that if the athletes pulled the plug on their voluntary contributions, the nation would have millions of seniors with no Social Security.

Social security made for good sound bites, and Joe Willie, now taking shots every day, was able to speak for five to seven minutes and appear coherent. Dwayne would then step up to field press questions. George Blair and Joe Willie were running in a dead heat in the daily polls.

Lillian picked up the rag and read Kipfer's latest column:

> *Could it be, America? That the Federalist candidate has a stormy past? Could it be that in high school he was a drunk, a womanizer, and maybe a rapist? Whoa. Now that is some story. Our sources tell us they know a woman who will verify that presidential nominee Joe Willie Benton was a truant and a drunk, and he forced her to have sex with him. Does that sound like a Friendly Federalist?*

"Dwayne, Joe Willie, you might want to take a look at this." Lillian tossed the paper on the coffee table between them. She had little doubt that the story was true. She wanted to be first lady, but she knew that sooner or later Joe Willie's past was going to come to light and nullify all she had endured as Lillian Benton.

#

Six months into the campaign, the smears heated up. The polls still held the two major candidates in a dead heat. Kipfer's articles threw equal amounts of dirt at each candidate. Joyce Unger continued to take a larger piece of the pie than expected. It would still not be enough to win, but enough to hurt one or both of the candidates in a close race.

George looked at his team of campaign leaders and his running mate, Ray Kennedy, all gathered in his Colorado war room.

"George, I think you need to call Unger. It's time to ask her, if she's going to concede, to give you her endorsement. The election is only four months away." Ray was pushing to get her out of the race so people could focus on two candidates.

"I think that's insulting and presumptuous. She's doing well. Why would she want to step down? Who says she doesn't support Joe Willie? No, it's too soon to ask for her endorsement." George knew he angered his campaign people by holding to principles, but he believed in old-fashioned ideals and wasn't ready to cave in to politics as usual.

"George, don't wait too long. I guarantee you the Federalists will be contacting her, if they haven't already." Ray paced the room, then came to sit next to George on the red leather sofa. "George, one week, and we have to move on this. I'll do it if you want me to. Then it won't look as if you're being egotistical."

"One week—and I'll do the calling," George snapped.

#

Ronald turned on the audio as he watched the surveillance camera planted in Joyce Unger's suite. Joyce sat with her campaign advisors, holding Cornell's hand, and proceeded to tell Barbara and her campaign workers the news they didn't want to hear. But it was the news Ronald wanted to hear. She was pulling out.

"No, it's too soon," Barbara said. "Joyce, you're coming up every day in the polls. You're making them squirm." Barbara was a savvy young white attorney, and she had led an aggressive but civil campaign. Ronald was pleased at how convincing she was during this crucial moment. She was good at her job.

"Barbara, it's over. It's not fair to the American people, and that's the only reason I want to stop. I'm going to call George Blair today and tell him."

"What? You're endorsing Blair?" Barbara was stunned.

Ronald glared at the screen. This was not what the Council wanted to hear. She was supposed to endorse Joe Willie.

"I am. Joe Willie is a loose cannon. The Federalists have some hidden agenda. I don't know what it is, but I don't like it."

"Joyce, you can't do that. The party will pitch a fit."

"I don't care. I'm calling George Blair right after my television announcement. I want you to arrange a press conference for four o'clock. That'll give Blair time to accept and hit the six o'clock news."

Barbara stood to leave and hugged Joyce. "I hope you know what you're doing." Ronald was again impressed by Barbara's acting ability.

Joyce hugged her back. "I know what I'm doing. Thanks, Barbara, for all you've done. I know this is hard, but it's for the best. Maybe in four years we'll try again."

#

Ronald threw his glass across the room of the lodge, and Chivas ran down the log siding. Unger was stepping down and would announce an endorsement at four o'clock. He called Samuel Gould. "Sam, can you get our people to sway her decision to endorse Blair? Can we switch her over to our man? If not, we need to get our hitter to her hotel."

"I'm on it. Call you right back."

Samuel dialed Barbara. She had been loyal and kept the Federalists apprized of Unger's every move. Ronald was not pleased with Samuel's return call.

"Barbara says no way. Unger is firm. She's going to endorse Blair."

"Very well." Ronald made the call.

#

The Council sat together in the lodge with Ronald and watched as Joyce made her way to the convention hall. She walked with great dignity, with Cornell and her children at her side. She had not been able to reach George Blair to tell him personally that she was endorsing him. Instead, he would hear it on PIC along with the rest of America.

Security was tight, but no one noticed a young man sipping a coke through a thin straw only a few feet away. No one noticed him when he lifted the straw and blew through it. Everyone noticed when Joyce Unger collapsed. The dart instantly sent poison to her central nervous system. Barbara had grabbed the speech notes from Joyce's hands before her body hit the floor.

#

Ronald and the Council continued to watch as Barbara went to the podium. She was composed and professional. "Ladies and gentlemen, it is my painful

270

duty to tell you that Congresswoman Joyce Unger was attacked just minutes ago by an assassin. We have no details other than she was shot with a poison dart." She paused dramatically in the ensuing silence. "I'm sad to say that the congresswoman has died."

Flash bulbs exploded. An uproar from the delegates, and the din of reporters shouting questions, all erupted from the floor at once. Barbara held her hands for silence, brushing false tears aside.

"My dear friend and leader is dead. She wanted to tell you—" She waved the speech notes in the air for them to see. "She wanted to tell you that because of her great love for the American people and our democratic process, she would step down so there could be a two-party vote. She wanted to tell you she felt there was only one person who could lead this great nation to glory, and that she wanted you, her supporters, to turn to the man she wished to endorse: Joe Willie Benton."

Ronald smiled and drained his glass. "Let's go get some fresh meat." He was already peeling out of his human costume.

$ $ $

271

CHAPTER TWENTY-EIGHT

After Joyce Unger's death, the two parties settled into vicious campaigning. Judy traveled with George, and on occasion the twins joined them. George hated using the twins for campaign purposes, but it served a two-fold mission: he got to spend time with them, and, after every appearance, he pulled ahead of Joe Willie in the polls.

Ray called from Washington. "George, can you set up Denver for an emergency meeting of all the western states' leaders?"

"Sure. Who, what, why, and when?" George was surprised by the request, coming so close to the end of the campaign.

"Every representative, congressman, senator, governor, and mayor from Montana, Wyoming, Utah, Idaho, Colorado, Arizona, New Mexico, Nevada, California, Oregon, and Washington. We've just run into a major problem, and if we don't fix it, the oil companies can start drilling anywhere and everywhere."

"What are you saying?"

"Bush slipped through a little bill that allows oil drilling anywhere in those states after January of next year. That means Rocky Mountain National Park, Yellowstone, Grand Canyon, Bryce Canyon, the national forests, Indian reservations, and so on. Get the picture? No place is exempt. The bastards can drill anywhere. We have to get a unanimous vote to repeal this bill immediately."

"Jesus, where has that little bill been hiding?"

"I think in Bush's safe deposit box. It's out now, and we have to get on it."

"I'll call Mayor Strauss in Denver and have him book as many hotels as he can. The overflow will have to shuttle from Colorado Springs." George scratched his head. *How could people be so damn greedy?* "Next Saturday soon enough?"

"Yep."

#

The convention hall was filled to overflowing, and every ballroom in the city and in Colorado Springs was packed. They were receiving the telecast live and were equipped to ask questions and receive answers via satellite. George addressed the group, and Judy stood in the rear of the room watching him. She had never seen him act under this kind of pressure. Sure, he had handled family crises and deaths, and he had done an admirable job in the Senate. But she puffed up with pride as she listened to him address this multi-partisan group. He had moved with lightning speed and efficiency setting up the meeting. Yes, her husband would make an exceptional president.

George pulled the party leaders together—Republicans, Democrats, Federalists, and Independents. They had to get the bill repealed immediately, or oil rigs were going to sprout up on every available square inch of the western states. Ray Kennedy assured him the sitting president would sign such a bill, even though he was just months from the end of his term.

Judy watched and was surprised when she heard a soft voice. "You really love him, don't you?"

She turned to look upon the lovely Lillian Benton. They had never met, but her striking face was easily recognizable. Judy smiled and took Lillian's hand in greeting.

"Does it show?"

"Oh yes, it does." Lillian continued to hold her hand. "Could we slip away somewhere for lunch?"

Judy was surprised, but the invitation sounded good. She and George hadn't eaten since yesterday evening, and he didn't need her right now. "Yes, let's do that."

The Maitre d' found them a private booth in the Brown Palace dining room. Judy ordered coffee for them both. She looked at Lillian and decided her beauty had not been exaggerated by the press.

Lillian took a sip of her coffee and smiled. "You probably think I'm nuts, but I just had this impulse to meet you and talk to you like two women, not political wives. Do you?"

"Do I what?"

"Think I'm crazy."

Judy laughed. "No, not at all. It's refreshing. This campaign is a real grind."

Lillian turned somber. "That it is. I was so surprised when I watched you watching George. You really love him, and in spite of this past year of every move being watched by the pollsters, the press, and the FBI—well, it's all there for you. I envy you."

Their chef's salads came. "What is it like to know everything about your husband?" Lillian asked before taking a bite.

"Well, I, uh… what do you mean?"

"Oh, silly stuff, like where he was born, who his parents are, stuff like that."

"I had forgotten, Joe Willie was adopted, wasn't he? Is that what you mean?"

Lillian held Judy's eyes with an intense look for a moment. Judy began to wonder if this meeting was so coincidental. Lillian looked at her plate. "I have no idea where he came from. It's as if he didn't exist before he came to the Bentons." She resumed drinking coffee, her salad forgotten.

Judy tried to change the subject. "Doesn't matter. He was in an orphanage, and the records were probably sealed."

"I don't think so. I hired a private detective, and he could find nothing." Lillian paused. "Well, listen to me babble on. I bet you have pictures of Matt and Martha. May I see them?"

Judy and Lillian finished lunch chit-chatting about family, the places they were traveling, and the pace of campaigning. Judy looked at her watch. "We'd better get back. The meeting will be breaking up. They probably didn't miss us. I enjoyed this visit."

"Me, too. I feel like you're my friend. Isn't that silly?"

"No, I feel that way, too. Maybe we can do this again." They stood and crossed the dining room. Other customers stared, surprised to see the two would-be first ladies dining together.

The meeting ended with a unanimous vote to stop the drilling and to repeal the Bush law that allowed such an affront to the land. Congress would pass the bill in an emergency session, and the president would sign it. The protected lands and national parks were once again safe from the corruption of the oil magnates.

$ $ $

CHAPTER TWENTY-NINE

George was holding a slight lead in the polls, and Kipfer had not burned him or Joe Willie for several days. George and Judy went from city to city, sometimes separately, sometimes together, and once in a while with the twins. George was enjoying a weekend in Colorado, resting and regrouping for the last frantic month of campaigning.

Sitting in his war room, he looked out the window toward Kansas. *By golly, George, I think you might pull it off. I want to be president. I can help people. I think I can make us a stronger, safer country.*

"Mr. Blair." Hilda had taken to calling him Mr. Blair since his father had passed away. He turned to answer, and suddenly he realized that Hilda had grown old. She now walked with a shuffle, and her back was rounded. He loved her, this lady who had been his second mother.

"What is it, Hilda?"

"There's a man here to see you. He won't tell me what he wants, and all he gave me for a name was Sam. He's so persistent, I can't get him to leave. He says it's of vital importance to the country that he see you. Do you want me to call security?"

George sighed mightily. Every fruitcake in the country had something of vital importance to tell him, and usually he just turned it over to security. Today, for some reason, he told Hilda to show the man in.

Sam was gray-haired, tall, and carried a small paunch. He walked erect and proud. He reached out a beefy hand that had seen years of hard work. "Mr. Blair, thank you for seeing me."

George shook the hand and looked into the steely gray eyes of a man he knew he could trust. "Sam, welcome. Hilda says you have something of importance to our country to share. Would you like a beer while we talk?"

"No, sir, I'll just say what I have to say and be on my way. I know you're busy. I do want you to win this election, because the alternative is too terrible to consider."

George motioned him to take a seat in the large green recliner, and then sat back on the sofa facing his visitor with his fingers steepled under his chin. He knew it was a power position; he did it to test the man.

"This man Joe Willie, he's a bad person," Sam began. "Several years ago, I owned a little cowboy bar outside Kingman, Arizona. My wife, well, she was my waitress then, and Joe Willie raped and beat her. He damn near killed her. She still has nightmares."

George held up his hand and leaned forward. "Sam, you look like an honest guy, but I can't be dealing with these kind of rumors. We don't pay to smear the opposition."

Sam's face turned red with anger. "I didn't come here for your damn money. Don't insult me. I been paid off once, and it damn near ruined my life. I'm telling you, that little shit raped my Dot. He beat her bloody and left her to die. We took hush money from the Bentons. Wish we hadn't, but we did. Never dreamed the asshole would get this far. Mr. Blair, he can't become president. You've got to stop him."

George went to the bar. Like his father, he thought better when he was pacing. He hit the intercom to the kitchen. "Hilda, is Ray still here?"

"Yes, I'm fixing him lunch. He's right here."

"Send him in."

George made the introductions, and this time Sam took his offer of a beer.

"Now tell Ray what you told me."

Sam repeated the story, only this time he recounted the accident that had followed the rape. "What's strange about the wreck is that according to my nephew, Joe Willie was a breath away from dying when they cleared the Sedona airport, and stories have it a spaceship lifted him off that mesa. When he came back, he was beat up, but alive. My nephew says no human could have survived that crash."

279

George and Ray glanced at each other. "Sam, forget the spaceship part. Can you prove the rape?"

"No sir, but Dot will go on television and identify him. Don't want no fame or money. We just want to make sure that animal don't get in the White House." Sam drained his beer.

Ray was grinning from ear to ear and started to speak, but George signaled him to wait.

"Sam, why didn't you come forward sooner? Why now?"

"We kept thinking it wasn't possible for that little shit to stay even with you. Now we're afraid he might buy his way in. He has to be stopped. I tell you, he's evil. There's something not of this Earth about him."

Sam and Dot were staying two nights at the Best Western off Garden of the Gods Road. Ray took their room and phone number and tried to give Sam some money, but Sam would have no part of it.

"We got him, George," Ray said after Sam had left. "We got him. Call Kipfer."

"No way. I'm not stooping to that. We've got no proof. And besides—spaceships? Christ, Ray, we'll be the ones on the losing end of that tale."

"What if it's true?"

"No, Ray, I said no. I win on my own merits. Thank you."

#

Judy, Martha, and Hilda looked like guilty children as they listened in on the intercom which Hilda had accidently left on. Judy called Alvin Lundquist. "I'm coming down. Get Kipfer on the line for a conference call."

She left the kitchen with a big grin on her face. Martha and Hilda smiled and poured another cup of coffee.

#

George reached over and found the bed empty. "Hey, Mrs. Blair, where are you? You can't ravish a man like that and then run off."

She came out of the bathroom, her blonde hair still wet from the shower. "Jesus, George, what a night. We haven't had that kind of sex for months. This home stretch seems to agree with you."

He buzzed the kitchen. "Hilda, we're going to enjoy a little more private time. How about coffee, juice and the papers?"

"Right away."

Hilda brought them everything he had asked for, plus two piping-hot, homemade cinnamon rolls. They sat on the bed and enjoyed the luxury. This afternoon they would be back on the plane for the final days of the campaign.

"You're up five points today." Judy smiled as she bit into the hot roll. "Oh my, almost as good as last night."

"I hope last night was better." George opened *What if America?* to Kipfer's column:

Could it be, America? That one of our presidential contenders raped and beat a woman in Kingman, Arizona? Could one of these men who wants to be president be a woman-beating rapist? It could be. This reporter has it on pretty good authority that one of them did beat and rape a waitress in Arizona.

To be continued next week...

$ $ $

CHAPTER THIRTY

P IC, the new political information channel, was not under the control of Samuel Gould's communication network, a fact that irritated Ronald.

They sat on the deck of the Baldpate, enjoying lunch in the fall air. Election day was just four weeks away, and Joe Willie was trailing forty-two percent to Blair's forty-eight percent. Ten percent were undecided. Someone had left a copy of *What if America?* on a chair, and Ronald flipped it open. His eyes caught Kipfer's latest story on the rape.

"Shit! Look at this." He threw the paper on the table and motioned the waiter for a check. "Goddamn it. Sam, you and I are on our way to Sedona. You too, Jackson. John, you and Richard find that double-crossing barkeep and his wife, and this time, make sure their silence is permanent."

283

He tossed bills on the table and, without waiting for a response, stormed out of the Baldpate. John and Richard gulped down their drinks and followed.

#

Ronald, Samuel Gould, Governor Benton, Jackson, Dwayne and Joe Willie sat in Benton's Sedona office, frantically trying to figure some way to stop the damage Kipfer's article could do.

"Look," Samuel said, "we've got the special to run a week before election, the one where the devoted son returned to be at his mother's bedside after she suffered her stroke, how he gave up a life at Harvard to love and care for her. We've got great shots of Lillian and him helping the poor and visiting the reservations. We can poke holes in Kipfer's stuff. Where is the proof? Only two living people know the real truth, right? We'll jump ahead and run all this stuff tonight and tomorrow."

Ronald was still steaming. He glared at Joe Willie. If he dared, he would remove his skin and tear the little son of a bitch apart. He went to the bar and poured a tumbler of Chivas, then crossed the room and bent over Joe Willie so his face was inches from his. He was sure Joe Willie could feel his hot breath. In a voice meant to intimidate, he said, "Joe Willie. You are not to utter one word that we haven't fed you. You are not to answer any reporters' questions. You go on stage, say what you're programmed to say, and get off. Do you understand?"

He turned to Dwayne. "And you. You stick to him like crazy glue. He doesn't take a crap without you."

Dwayne smirked.

"Get serious, Dwayne. We're going to jump on the plight of rape victims everywhere. The things this administration will do to see that such a thing never happens to another American woman. This is a new issue, and by God, we'll turn it into a benefit."

"Let's get Lillian to visit all the rape centers she can in the next two days. Homes for battered women, too." Samuel was excited. "We can turn this into a positive issue. Look at how outraged our candidate is." Samuel pointed to Joe Willie, who stared back blankly.

The next morning, Ronald watched the polls on PIC. He was angry over the breaking news, which now gave Joe Willie a slim thirty-five percent and George Blair sixty percent, with five percent undecided. "Samuel, get on damage control. I want that Harvard sob story on every damn network you own tonight and in every morning paper."

Samuel went to the phone and started sending faxes and making calls. Tonight, America would fall in love with the devoted son. Tomorrow, the outrage campaign would begin with the new mantra "Federalists Fight for Rape Victims."

"Jackson, get Lillian started immediately with visits to battered women's shelters. Schedule her some speeches on stiffer sentences for rapists, and get her on all the talking head shows. Move it!"

#

Joe Willie sat in the big leather chair as far away from the group as he could get. His headaches were getting worse. Every day, Carl shot him full of something. For about twenty minutes he would feel really good, clear of mind, talking brilliantly and giving his speech. Then he became sleepy and would nod off no matter where he was. Right now he was so tired, he could barely make out what they were saying.

I wish I could just take a horse and ride up to Studder's and Devil Dog's graves. They would understand. Even Pres would understand. I don't think I can take much more of this.

"Do you hear me, Joe Willie?" Ronald was in his face again.

"Yeah, I hear. I'll do whatever it takes, just let me rest for awhile. I'm so tired."

"Fuck you. You can rest once you're elected. Four more weeks, and the issue is women. 'How could anyone do that to a woman?' Got it?"

Joe Willie nodded and drifted off.

#

The Colorado Springs nightly news was interrupted by a breaking news story:

Two bodies were found today off Gold Camp Road. A man thought to be about sixty-five and a woman of about the same age were pulled from their car, which evidently missed a curve and rolled to the bottom of a ravine. The bodies were discovered by hikers. The cause of death is still undetermined. The coroner said the throats had been ripped open, as if by an animal, and their blood had been drained. This is not the work of a cougar or wolf, the coroner stated. We'll give you more details as we receive them.

The station cut to a commercial, then resumed the local broadcast.

#

Joe Willie went to his room to rest. Ronald, Jackson, Samuel, and Dwayne continued their meeting. They had asked Governor Benton to leave them. Benton had served his purpose years before and was no longer an asset. Besides, they didn't want him hearing everything they needed to discuss.

"Dwayne, you've got to keep Joe Willie out of trouble. Take over as much as you can, without making him look totally helpless. Can you handle it?"

"Sure. Let me suggest that Carl cut back on the medication. Joe Willie's brain is fried. Remember how well he was doing during his second Senate bid? He was damn near human. Could you get him back to that? I can handle the cameras and stuff, but he needs some relief. He's going to crack if you keep pushing him."

Ronald never liked to be corrected, but he could see that his candidate was a zombie. He rang for Carl.

While they were meeting to discuss a way to mellow out their puppet, a black dust-covered Chevy pulled up in front of the house. Ronald could see a plump platinum blonde and a boy of about sixteen or seventeen exit the car. Benton went out to meet them. Ronald wondered who the hell this frump was and what grief she was bringing. They went up the steps and out of his sight.

"Can you do it?" he asked Carl.

"He'll never be the way he was. There are just too many chemicals, too much damage. But I think I can bring him closer to normal. He needs a complete break from the drugs."

"Can't do that, Carl. Fix him the best you can. We only have four more weeks to go, then two months before he's inaugurated. Keep him together. Avery says the planet is in bad shape. We have to get our lab down here soon, or we'll lose everything." He refilled his glass. "We could use a break."

"Why don't I implant another chip? Then I could cut back on the drugs."

"Do it." Ronald was feeling the pressure. They had to win this election, or Nefaz was doomed.

Ronald would sacrifice anyone to win. His life and his planet's race depended on winning.

An aide opened the door and poked his head into the room. "Excuse me, but this lady won't go away," he said, trying to keep the frumpy blonde from bulldozing her way in. "She says she has information that will win the election for Joe Willie."

"Oh hell, why not? Nothing else is going right. Show her in."

Evelyn's plump body and blonde hair were immediately distasteful to Ronald. He was amused as he watched Dwayne, ever ingratiating, go to greet her. "Welcome, I'm Dwayne Rogers. And you are?"

She smiled coyly and wiggled her ample hips suggestively. "Oh, I know who you are. I'm soooo pleased to meet you. I'm Evelyn Jones, and this is my son, George junior."

Ronald dropped his glass. *There is a god on this planet.*

Walking quickly to her, he took her hand in both of his. "Evelyn, welcome. Please sit. What would you like to drink?" He led her to the red sofa and turned to shake the boy's hand. "George junior. What a coincidence. Our opponent's name is George. Any connection?"

"This is George Blair's son."

Ronald could barely contain his excitement. *They had the son of a bitch now*. "You have proof?"

Evelyn hesitated momentarily. "For the right price, I can get proof."

"One million. Will that work for you?"

"Why, no, we had in mind more like five." She batted her eyelashes and motioned George junior to come sit beside her. He was the right age, and with his dark eyes and brown hair, he resembled Blair.

Ronald had neither the time nor the patience to play with this whore, but if what she said was true…

"Three and a half as soon as you provide proof."

Evelyn turned all business. "Proof or not, the rumor will hurt him. Two million now for our signed statements and pictures, two million more when you get the DNA results."

#

Judy was in her office having coffee with Alvin. They were pleased with the poll results. She was going to travel with George for the final push, and the twins would accompany them. They were going to win. She could feel it. She and Alvin had done all they could in the smear campaign, and so far George knew nothing about her participation in the seedy end of the campaign.

"I think we got it, Alvin. My ESP says so. George gets stronger as he enters the final stretch. Family values, honesty, great insight into what is needed to make America great… I just don't see what could go wrong."

Alvin was about to answer when his secretary opened the door. "I hate to disturb you, but you need to see this." She handed Alvin a *What if America?* magazine, already opened to Kipfer's column:

> *Could it be, America, that the all-American family has a rather large sixteen-year-old skeleton in its closet?*
>
> *According to my sources, a leading political candidate has an illegitimate sixteen-year-old son. According to sources, the candidate thought there had been an abortion. Mr. Family Values hoped his past would never come alive. But it seems that his past, and perhaps a bastard son, is very much alive.*
>
> *Could it be, America, that we are about to elect a man who has lied to us? Makes you wonder what else he might have lied about, doesn't it?*

Alvin looked at the picture of Evelyn and her son as he read the article twice, then passed it over to Judy. She read and reread. She felt her anger grow so intense, she was numb. She spoke icily, "I'll take this. I'm going home, Alvin."

"Judy, I know that voice. Please stay here a moment. Let's talk this through."

She was already on her way out the door. "There is nothing to discuss. If this is true, I will divorce him right in the middle of his campaign." Her voice broke, and she felt tears coming to the surface. She jerked open the door and ran out of the office.

When she got home, she threw open the door of the war room and tossed the magazine on George's desk. "You son of a bitch! You and Evelyn conceived a baby? You tried to get it aborted? You lied to me. You've been lying to me all these years. Is this true?" The campaign committee members scurried for exits.

George jumped up and tried to take her in her arms. "Judy, wait just a minute."

She had never thought she could hate him, but at this moment she wanted to hurt him, to lash out and make him feel her pain. She spun around and ran up the stairs to their bedroom. George came right behind her.

"Judy, wait."

"Get away from me. I hate you." The door slammed in his face, sending two pictures jumping from the wall in the hallway.

He knocked tentatively before entering. Judy stood in the center of the room, shaking and sobbing. She had pulled a suitcase out of the closet, and now she started throwing in her clothes.

"Judy, please. Let me tell you what happened."

She wanted to hear him out, but she was so hurt. She turned and was ready to lash out again when Matt and Martha peeked in the open doorway.

"What's wrong?" Matt asked. "We heard swearing and fighting." Martha stood wide-eyed and frightened. George took them into the hall and closed the door.

Judy could hear him comforting them. "It's okay. Mommy and I had a misunderstanding. I want you to go find Grandma. I'll be down shortly. Mommy and I need to clear this up."

"Is she all right?" Martha asked.

"She'll be fine. Go on now, find Hilda and Grandma."

Judy locked the door and continued packing. George knocked and knocked, but she refused to open the door.

A short time later, Judy heard a soft tap and the gentle voice of her mother-in-law. "Judy, let me in."

She had come to love Martha and considered her a second mother. She unlocked the door, and they embraced. Judy knew her eyes were red and puffy from crying. She went to the bed and sat next to the half-packed suitcase. Martha sat beside her and held her hand.

"Judy, you can't leave." Her touch and her voice were soft and comforting.

"Martha, I have to. I can't be with a man who would lie and cover up having a son. He never even told me. He never told me he had gotten her pregnant. I'll divorce him. I'm sorry, I can't love him ever again."

"Yes, you can, and yes, you will. We don't even know if the boy is his. Lawyers are preparing a libel suit against Miss Jones, the magazine, and probably Joe Willie's campaign leaders. There is no proof. We are demanding an immediate DNA test."

Judy brightened a bit. Perhaps it wasn't George's son, but then, why had he never told her about the pregnancy? "I still—well, he lied. He was unfaithful, and I won't be lied to."

Martha was firm in her response, loving but unyielding. "Grow up, Judy. We all make mistakes. This marriage is not about your feelings, it's about being the wife of a powerful leader. He will be president, and you will not divorce him."

Judy was surprised at the stern response. She looked at Martha and saw her in a new light. She had never realized that Martha was such a powerful woman, that it was quiet Martha who had masterminded the Blair legacy. She never thought how Martha might have watched her husband cheat, lie, and God knows what else. She saw a woman she would have to emulate.

Sheepishly, she replied, "I get it. I'm still angry, but I'll stay. I never realized I have a duty to the American people, too. It isn't about me any longer, is it?"

Martha patted her hand again. "No dear, it never was about you. Put your suitcase away, and come have coffee with me. I sent George away for a few hours. You can talk to him later."

Judy sighed. She knew her place, and she felt suddenly very mature. She had to remember how she and Alvin connived and fed dirt to Kipfer. She had used smear tactics when George forbade it. Maybe she had lied, too. Maybe some things were better left unsaid to a spouse. She knew she had reached a milestone in their relationship.

$ $ $

CHAPTER THIRTY-ONE

Joe Willie had been drug-free for a week, functioning better with the new microchip Carl had implanted. Now, with only three weeks until election day, he was feeling better. He was glad the Federalists had let Dwayne and Lillian lead the campaign by speaking out for rape victims. The rape story had never been proven. No one had come forward to fuel the rumor that Joe Willie had raped the woman. He was tickled by the Blair story. It had everyone's attention, and Samuel made sure his stations and papers carried news every day of the illegitimate son.

Joe Willie had even found a few hours to take Pres and ride up to the graves. He was always comforted by talking to his deceased buddies. Today he would have to get back on the campaign trail. He was leading in the PIC polls sixty percent to Blair's thirty-five.

"Hey, Mr. President, you ready?" Dwayne's voice shook him out of his reverie.

"I'm ready."

Joe Willie, Ronald, Lillian, Dwayne, and Carl climbed into the black limousine. With the secret service following, they began a sweep of the country. Three weeks to go, and if their luck held, Joe Willie would be the winner by a landslide.

He smiled as he looked out at the familiar sandstone sculptures. President Joe Willie Benton. Sounded good to him.

#

George put his feet up on the coffee table as he watched the PIC polls. It didn't look good. Judy was civil to him in private, warm and loving in public. Traveling with his family helped his image, but he wasn't coming up in the polls as quickly as they had hoped. He stayed on target with national issues and programs, steering clear of family values and abortion.

Ray Kennedy burst into the room, waving a piece of paper. "Hot damn, partner, we're back in business! Here's the DNA report, and there isn't a chance in a zillion that boy is yours."

George grabbed the report and read it quickly. The PIC station broke for breaking news.

"This just in, confirmed information. DNA absolutely disproves the claim of an illegitimate son for George Blair. It is not true. Let me say it again, presidential candidate George Blair does not have an illegitimate son. We are expecting word from the Democratic campaign manager momentarily."

Judy came from the bedroom and went into George's arms. He held her tightly and felt her warmth. She looked up with blue eyes and said softly, "I'm so sorry. Forgive me."

"No need. We have work to do." He turned to Ray. "I want a press conference. I'll take this one. The people deserve to hear it from me, not the campaign manager."

#

One week to election, George had closed the gap in the polls but still trailed Joe Willie by five points. Now the pundits were saying it was too close to call. Ronald called the governor of California, a loyal Federalist. "Governor, whatever it takes, we have to carry California. Do you have the polls fixed to do so?"

"We'll make it happen if it gets that close. Don't worry."

Ronald hung up and read a small column that said airport officials in the Caymans had spotted a woman who resembled Evelyn Jones traveling with her son. What a bitch. She had taken the two million and run, knowing full well the boy wasn't Blair's. Well, after the election, someone would visit Ms. Jones in the Caymans.

#

Two days before the election, Judy was dressing for an evening of television. She and George had appearances on two prime-time talk shows scheduled tonight, neither station belonging to Samuel Gould. Joe Willie and Dwayne were appearing on Gould's networks and at a Willie's Women rally.

PIC was calling the numbers forty-eight to forty-eight. Judy listened to them drone on in the background. "George, do you know where Joe Willie was born?"

"No, and I don't particularly care." He hollered from the bathroom. "Why on Earth are you asking me?"

"When I had lunch with Lillian in Denver, she mentioned that she didn't know where he was born. Wouldn't it be interesting to see his birth certificate?"

George came out of the bathroom wrapped in a towel. "What are you getting at?"

"What if he doesn't have a birth certificate? He can't be president if he can't prove citizenship, right?"

George let the towel drop and ran to the phone. "Ray, get someone on this right away. We want to see Joe Willie's birth certificate."

Judy smiled at her naked husband. "Too bad we don't have some spare time."

George laughed, picked up his towel and snapped her with it on his way to the bathroom.

#

The day before the election, *What if America?* carried this piece:

> *Could it be, America, that we have a man running for president who cannot prove his citizenship? Could it be that one of the two front-runners will have to concede because he cannot prove his birthright to hold the highest office in the land? Hold on America, this could get interesting!*

Before noon, every paper, every radio station, and every television channel was on the story. Joe Willie Benton could not prove his citizenship. He would have to step out of the race.

#

Joe Willie, Dwayne, and Lillian sat in stunned silence in the governor's office in Sedona, listening to the reporter. Joe Willie had come to believe he would win. Lillian and Dwayne would be with him, and his life would finally be perfect.

The Federalist leader called. "Joe Willie, you have to go on television and pull out of the race."

Joe Willie was tired of taking orders. "You do it. I quit."

Dwayne stared at the television.

Lillian panicked and ran out of the room.

Joe Willie followed her to the bedroom, where he kicked off his black dress shoes and quickly escaped the suit and tie. In seconds he had on his faded Levi's, ragged blue shirt, and boots.

"Lillian, stay with me," Joe Willie pleaded. Gone was the smug egotistical man of an hour before.

Her heart went out to him. He was so pathetic, like an ugly dog who had just rolled in manure but thought you would like nothing better than to pet him. She thought of Tom, wishing she had gone with him. She would rather have died with him than live any longer with Joe Willie.

"I can't," she said. "I just can't. We were never in love. We had a contract. The contract just got canceled." Pulling down her travel bag, she began putting in a few things. She would come back to get the rest later.

A howl came from Joe Willie as he curled up in a ball on the floor, more animal than man. He wailed and sobbed as she finished packing and walked out of his life.

Joe Willie dragged himself off the floor and went to the cabinet in Carl's room where Carl kept the serums. Carefully he filled the black bag with all the vials and syringes, then sneaked quietly out the back door to the corral. As he saddled Jeb's old roping horse, he saw Dwayne toss his suitcase in the backseat of Lillian's red Mercedes. He felt absolutely betrayed as he watched the two of them speed off down the dirt road.

Pres came to him happily, barking and wagging his tail. "You're getting old, Pres," Joe Willie said. "All white around the nose."

He tied the black bag on the back of the saddle and started up the trail beside the sometime creek, unaware of the colorful fall orange and red leaves. He could barely see for the tears that gushed down his cheeks.

Pres chased happily after him. "We're gonna go see Studder and Devil Dog. To hell with all of them. I didn't want to be president anyway."

He knew the long ride would be too much for Pres, so he laid the dog in front of the saddle, the place where he had ridden for many years.

When they arrived at the graves, Joe Willie sat on the red sand between the two markers and opened Carl's bag. "You want me to take shots, Ronald?" he screamed at the sky. "I'll take your damned shots!"

He picked a vial at random, filled the syringe, and jammed the needle into his thigh. He felt the familiar change of mood, but through the haze he kept his mind focused on his mission. His life had been all about the shots and the moods. He picked another vial, filled it, and jammed it into his leg. Pres sat and watched.

"I love you, Pres, but I'm going to join Studder and Devil Dog. You'll come soon." He patted his friend's head and reached for another vial. He was feeling strange as he continued to shoot himself with vial after vial of mood serums.

Later that evening, Carl found Joe Willie sprawled across the graves of Studder and Devil Dog. Pres sat beside him, guarding the body.

#

Preceded by his anger, Ronald stormed to the bar. He was the last man to enter the lodge. Booze sloshed over his glass as he turned the bottle upside down. Adding no ice, he downed half a glass. He had picked up the damnable human habit of drinking when he was angry. He had been living among them too many years.

Sitting on the sofas with jackets off, ties loosened or thrown on the floor, were the remaining four members of the Power Council, stunned by their defeat. They had lost their attempt to buy Joe Willie the presidency.

Samuel Gould was head of the corporation which held controlling interest in communications. He monopolized television networks and major newspapers throughout the U.S. and Canada. He had made sure every tidbit of news was slanted to make George Blair look unfavorable. Likewise, all news had been construed to make Joe Willie look good. When it was leaked that there might have been a rape in Joe Willie's past, he had been able to turn the rape leak into a positive campaign issue.

Everything on the airways and in print had been controlled by Gould. Many reporters had lost their jobs this year because of a slip of the tongue. Gould had allowed no reporting that painted his rivals as remotely good. He had masterminded subliminal messages, which helped turn public opinion in their favor.

He could not believe they had failed, and on such a moronic oversight. They could have faked a damned birth certificate. Still, the leak was out, and it had hit the airwaves and print before he could stop it. Once out, it was all over. Joe Willie was not a citizen.

John Woods controlled oil. Nothing happened with oil, anywhere, without his okay. He manipulated the stock market, controlled oil prices, lifted embargos. He conspired to make the Blair party look fiscally unstable. Joe Willie had looked like a genius in finance when he was able to predict the oil trade per barrel increase. Jesus, how could they have failed? John was still shaking his head in disbelief.

Universal control of the food supply, farming, processing, and marketing belonged to Richard Rollins. He controlled or owned an interest in every major food company in the world. On his word, soybean stock rose or fell. He oversaw or had an interest in any merger or takeover. He was capable of stopping the world from eating, and yet they had been unable to stop the truth from leaking and ruining their world takeover.

Christ, Joe Willie had been an almost perfect puppet, with no brains or ambition of his own. He could be controlled with a shot from Carl or a trip back to Dr. Avery for some fine-tuning.

So intelligent, so compulsively needing to control, Jackson Ingersol slouched in the plush leather chair facing Richard Rollins. They were ruined. His skill at hacking into Democratic high level programs had kept them two jumps ahead throughout the election year. They couldn't move without his party knowing it ahead of time. They had out-maneuvered the opposition every step of the way. How could they have been so stupid as to forget a birth certificate? Ingersol was in control of the worldwide web, owner of a monopoly in the computer technology field, and his research and development dominated software development.

These five men controlled sixty percent of the world's wealth. They had unadulterated power. With Joe Willie as president, the long-time dream of the people of Nefaz to capture Earth would have been a reality. Now they had to accept failure.

Ronald finished his tumbler of bourbon, motioning John and Samuel to join the group. "We might as well get comfortable." Ronald kicked free of his shoes, toe to heel twice. His gorilla toes were relieved to be free of the cumbersome human shoes. His four companions followed his lead. Now all five men were sitting with their hairy feet free of shoes.

"Hell, let's get real comfortable." Richard grabbed the skin of his forehead and pulled downward. The human face peeled away, and he threw it across the room. His hairy brown face twisted into a grimace. His ape-like mouth twitched with anger.

The others joined him in peeling their human masks away. Now they were themselves, devil animals from Nefaz, animals resembling small Sasquatch.

#

George Blair sat in the oval office on his first day as president of the United States. The White House was buzzing as his family was moved in and signs of the former administration were moved out.

A pretty brunette aide in a very short skirt came in. She sat without being asked, and provided him a view. He felt himself come erect.

"Mr. President, I'm one of your aides, Bridget Maxwell. If there is anything you want, I mean anything, you let me know." She batted her heavily painted eyelashes.

George pushed the button for his personal secretary, and she entered immediately. "Mary, I'd like you to assign Bridget to Mrs. Blair."

Bridget's cheeks flushed with anger as Mary escorted her out of the office. Mary returned a moment later, smiling. "Is there anything else, Mr. President?"

"Yes, be sure I'm never alone anywhere, in any room of the White House, with any woman except my wife."

"Yes, sir." She closed the door and left him alone.

"Nice place, kiddo."

"Goddamn it, Matt, stop it."

"It's not nice to swear at your brother and your father."

"Dad, you here too?"

"Yes. I wanted to tell you I love you, and I'm very proud of you, son."

They were gone. He knew it would be many years before he heard from them again. He no longer needed anyone else's approval. He was his own man, President George Blair.

$ $ $